YOUR HAND *in* *Love*

YOUR HAND
in *Love*

Bettina Luxon

Linda Dearsley

CHANCELLOR
PRESS

First published in 1989 by Rosters Ltd

This edition published in 1995 by Chancellor Press
an imprint of Reed Consumer Books Ltd
Michelin House, 81 Fulham Road, London SW3 6RB
and Auckland, Melbourne, Singapore and Toronto

Copyright © Bettina Luxon & Linda Dearsley

ISBN 1 85152 709 5

A CIP catalogue is available for this book from the British Library

Printed in Great Britain by Bath Press

Acknowledgment

With special thanks to Julia, John, Breda and Paul, Beverley , Helen and John and Leslie, and everyone else who so kindly contributed to this book.

I would also like to thank my editor Rosemary for her unfailing patience, good advice and constant encouragement.

Bettina Luxon 1989

Contents

CHAPTER ONE:
THE COURSE OF LOVE

Looking back, Julia Lloyd realises she should have been suspicious. After all, it was so out of character.

'You're looking tired, you could do with a break,' said her husband, all consideration and gentle tones. 'You've always wanted to visit your sister in Africa – why don't you go. It'd do you the world of good.'

He even came home one day and presented her with the tickets. That really should have set the alarm bells ringing but Julia was so pleased they were getting on well that she squashed her doubts. She packed her prettiest summer clothes, promised to write and set off for the holiday of a lifetime.

It was a wonderful holiday as it turned out, which was just as well because it was the last carefree holiday she was to enjoy for years. She returned to find that her husband had moved another woman into the house during her absence. Before she'd even unpacked her case her marriage was over and her life was in ruins. Her husband walked out and Julia was left alone with three young children to bring up as best she could.

At first she was in shock. The devastating change in her life had come about so suddenly, so unexpectedly, that she felt quite numb. But then as sensation returned, depression set in. Miserable, broke and rejected, Julia felt as if her life was over. Then she saw a magazine

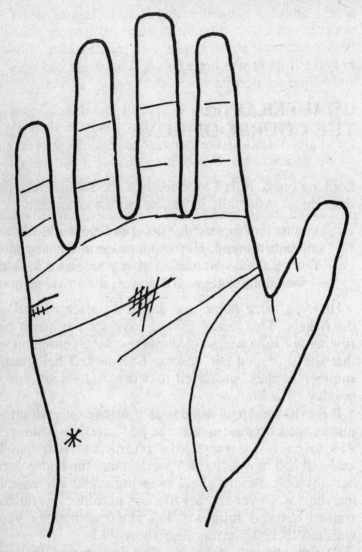

Julia

article about a palmist called Bettina Luxon. Julia had never given much thought to such exotica as palmistry before but now she was ready to try anything. She had to know if there was hope ahead. That night she sat down and wrote to Bettina.

'It sounds crazy now because I had the children and I loved them,' said Julia, 'but I was in such a state I felt I could have committed suicide. I even rang the Samaritans. To me it seemed as if everything had come to an end. I really needed to know if there was anything ahead to make life worth living. Bettina asked me to send photocopies of my hands. I found a photocopying machine (a lot of libraries have them) and sent the copies off. I was quite amazed at the report Bettina sent back. She was able to tell me that my husband had gone off with another woman, she even described her appearance and occupation correctly! She said that I was at rock bottom now but that things would be a lot brighter soon. I would marry again she said, but not for a few years yet. Everything she said was so right I felt very much encouraged.'

Over the next few years Julia sent Bettina several more photocopies of her hands.

'Each time I was more astonished' she said. 'Bettina told me that I was going to meet a self-employed man who was balding, with grey sideburns. He was a very caring, sensitive man she said and he was comfortably off.'

Shortly after this Julia met John who was an insurance broker. He fitted the description perfectly. Bettina went on to tell her that John was the right man for her and that he would give her a ruby and diamond ring. This seemed highly unlikely.

11

YOUR HAND IN LOVE

'I didn't think we were at that stage of our relationship' said Julia, 'but shortly afterwards John took me to the Ladbroke Hotel and proposed. I accepted and he brought out of his pocket this beautiful ring — a ruby surrounded by diamonds. We've been married four years now and I'm happier than I've ever been in my life. I don't know how Bettina does it but we're both amazed and thankful.'

Bettina Luxon finds it all quite natural. Palmistry is not an old superstition, she says, but a precise science which has to be studied like any other science. An accomplished palmist she believes, can tell almost anything about a person's past, present and future simply by examining their hands.

Bettina has been studying palmistry for 25 years but her interest in hands and the many fascinating lines etched on them goes back to her wartime childhood when she used to amuse herself during the long dismal nights in the air-raid shelter by drawing round her fingers. She quickly noticed that everyone's hands were different and she begged the other shelterers to allow her to copy their 'lines' on to the outlined palm she'd drawn. Unwittingly the young Bettina had stumbled on to one of the basic truths of palmistry.

'No two hands are the same,' said Bettina. 'Just as no two sets of finger prints are exactly alike. The hand is as individual as the personality and when you know what you are looking for you can read a person's character in minutes, just by studying their palm.'

When Bettina received Julia's photocopy hand prints she examined them carefully under a strong light.

'I saw that Julia would marry twice,' she said, 'because she had two marriage lines on the side of her hand. One of these, the top line, was strong and deep showing that the later marriage would be happy, but the lower line was shallow and surrounded by little criss cross lines like a chequer board. These are known as stress lines and their presence told me that Julia's first marriage was causing her a lot of worry. There were more stress lines around the heart line too, reinforcing the fact that her problems were emotional. Yet when I looked down her hand towards it's base, the criss cross lines cleared away and her palm looked clearer and smoother. This told me that life would improve for Julia as time went on.'

At intervals over the next few years Julia sent more photocopies.

'What most people don't realise,' said Bettina, 'is that the small lines on the hand change — often every three months as the circumstances in your life change. So it's not worth examining your own hand or going to a palmist too frequently but it might be useful to have a reading on a quarterly basis. As the months went on I noticed changes in Julia's hand. I saw the lines that revealed a new man about to come into her life along with the marks that showed he would be self-employed or run his own business. At the same time a star had appeared down near the base of Julia's hand. This told me that money and a comfortable life were on their way. The two things were clearly connected.'

Bettina does admit of course that she knows of no lines to foretell a ruby and diamond ring. This is where logic gives way to cloudier issues. Bettina is also psychic and sometimes when she is reading a hand she sees a psychic 'picture' as well as the physical lines. The details of Julia's ring came to her psychically and not through palmistry. Yet the two things are connected, she says.

'You don't have to be psychic to read hands,' said Bettina, 'anyone can learn to do it, although to get beyond the basics you need a great deal of patience and practice. The more hands you see the more clear the fundamental rules become and the less likely you are to confuse one line with another. Everyone has some degree of psychic ability or intuition, call it what you will. I believe that it's a left-over sense, a primitive sixth sense if you like, that's fallen into disuse in our sophisticated modern world.

'Some people have more ability than others just as some people have sharper vision or a keener sense of smell. Yet just like a muscle, the more you use this power the more it develops. When you are reading hands you're not consciously drawing on your psychic power but you are using it nevertheless and the more you use it the better it becomes. When you've been reading hands for a while you'll notice that you start getting very strong hunches about people that turn out to be correct. That is just the beginning.'

However, Bettina doesn't see palmistry as merely an exercise by which to develop latent talents. She believes that even in its most basic form the study of palmistry can help people improve just about every area of their lives.

'If Julia had been able to study and understand her own hand and that of her first husband before they married, she might have cancelled the wedding and saved herself a lot of heartache,' said Bettina, 'It's a pity that so many people only turn to palmistry when something's gone wrong in their lives. I would like to change all that.'

That's what this book is all about. Palmistry can help to improve your love life and save you a lot of problems. Of course, reading one book won't turn you into an expert palmist overnight but it will give you a lot of valuable information which you can use every single day of your life.

CHAPTER TWO:
DON'T BE FOOLED

Grandma's been warning us for years. 'Beauty is only skin deep,' she says. 'Handsome is as handsome does.' 'You can't tell a book by its cover.' And so on and so on. The same boring old clichés we've heard a thousand times before. Yet clichés are only clichés because they're true – as generations of lovers have found to their cost. Sparkling eyes and lovely features do not necessarily reflect a warm and caring heart. Good looks can just as easily conceal a cold and selfish nature. In fact, a handsome face is the perfect disguise and attractive people can often get away with the kind of behaviour that wouldn't be tolerated in their plainer brothers and sisters.

We all know this of course. We all know we shouldn't judge a book by its cover but in the absence of any other method by which to judge it, what else are we supposed to do? And if the cover happens to be unusually beguiling – well, is it any wonder we're taken in? Some people go from heartbreak to heartbreak picking the wrong partner every time and not finding out until it's too late.

> 'He seemed so nice, so genuine,' sobbed a young client of mine recently. 'He was good looking, he made me laugh and he was so polite. His manners were perfect. He wasn't like all the others.'

It was only after she gave up her job and flat to move nearer to him that she discovered the little matter he'd 'forgotten' to mention. He was married with two children and another baby on the way and had no intention of changing his life. I've lost count of the number of similar tales I've heard over the years.

Yet we don't have to put up with these harrowing experiences. We don't have to be helpless. There is a method by which you can learn a person's character in a few minutes and that method is as old as the oldest clichés. It is, of course, palmistry. By studying the most basic rules of palmistry you can tell at a glance whether a person is loving or selfish, whether they are generous or mean, brutal or caring. You can detect their sexual preferences, discover whether they are honest or born liars. You can even see whether they will make a good marriage partner.

Once you start looking at hands you'll be amazed to notice how often the hands and face fail to match up. Some of the loveliest movie stars have ugly, claw-like hands which look so out of place you'd think they belonged to someone else. The worst hands I've ever seen belonged to the most beautiful client ever to walk through my door. I've seen many many pretty girls of course but this one was exquisite. She had huge dark eyes, a lovely oval face, and long black hair that fell almost to her waist. She was tall and slender and immaculately dressed in an elegant suit of palest beige. Everything she wore toned, right down to her shoes, bag and gloves.

Gloves. It's unusual these days to see a woman wearing gloves in early summer unless she's going to a wedding, but as the girl peeled them off with a graceful, flowing movement I suddenly realised why she wore them. Her hands were appalling. Heavy, twisted and misshapen, it made me go cold just to look at them. How she got her gloves on over those crooked fingers I'll never know. Perhaps she had them specially made.

Swallowing my distaste I attempted to read her palm,

but tactful as I tried to be, I couldn't find anything good to say. I could see that she had a cruel, selfish nature and there was some unpleasantness in the past concerning a child which I didn't think I wanted to know about.

'I'm afraid that in the past you've let a child down badly,' I told her and I went on to mention a few other facts, well watered down with diplomacy.

The young woman was not at all pleased. After a few moments she snatched her hands away and furiously dragged on her gloves.

'You haven't told me anything I don't already know,' she spat angrily. 'If I'd known you could see that sort of thing I would never have come.'

And with that she jumped up, slammed out of the flat and went clattering away down the stairs. I've never been so glad to see the back of someone in my life.

But if ugly hands betray an ugly nature, take care before jumping to conclusions about beautiful hands. Those excessively narrow, pointed hands so beloved of artists are not necessarily beautiful to a palmist. I would much rather see a more substantial palm with straight, even fingers and a well developed, though not heavy, thumb.

As I've explained, palmistry can provide you with a great deal of vital information about a prospective partner but it can also tell you a lot about yourself. As well as indicating the strengths and weaknesses in your character it can show you whether you will have a happy marriage, whether you'll marry more than once, whether a divorce is likely and even the number of children you will have. Perhaps even more importantly, it can show you whether a prospective partner is truly compatible. Using the basic rules of palmistry you might well find a lover who is kind, honest and true − and yet you could still come unstuck. You could be incompatible in a hundred different ways.

One of you might be excessively tidy, the other a slob. One a spender, the other a thrifty soul and on a more serious level, you could get on well as people and yet find yourselves incompatible sexually — a surprisingly common problem.

The first steps

Most people start, for obvious reasons, by studying their own palm. This is a good idea as long as you go about it correctly. Watch anyone pick up a book on palmistry for the first time and you'll notice them immediately hold up their own hand to compare it with the diagrams on the pages. This is understandable but wrong. A palmist studies a hand from the fingertips up. If you hold your own hand in front of your face you are seeing it upside down from the palmistry point of view. But turn it round and the lines become distorted.

The only successful way to read your own hand is to make a print of your palm. The simplest way to do this is to take a photocopy of your hand. It's easily done. You place your hand, palm down on the machine, press the button with the other hand and wait while the copy is taken. But do make sure that the print is neither too dark nor too light. I've seen photocopied hand prints so dark you can't make out the lines on them.

These days most libraries have photocopying machines but if you live too far away from a machine or your nearest machine is out of order, you don't have to give up. The alternative is messy but effective. Take an old lipstick and rub it all over your hand until the palm and fingers are completely covered with colour. Then press your hand on to a sheet of clean white paper. When you lift it you should find a perfect print showing every line and detail of your palm.

The basics

When new clients come to me they always ask whether I want the right or the left palm. 'Neither,' I say, 'I want to see both,' and they are surprised when I study the shape of both hands, the length and texture of the fingers and the springiness of the thumb instead of getting down to what they consider the proper business of examining the lines.

The lines are very important, of course — they can tell you the minute individual details of a person's character, but it's not always possible to hold a subject's hand — especially when you don't want them to know that you are assessing them. This is where the shape of the hands and fingers is so useful. By studying the outline of the hand you can learn the broad outline of the personality and you can do this, undetected, simply by watching the subject pick up a glass, lift a cigarette, take notes from a wallet.

First of all consider the overall appearance of the hand, the colour, size and depth and the look of the nails.

● Red hands

When the hands, including the palms, are a deep and even red this denotes a passionate and sensuous nature. Less lusty types should steer clear of a partner with very red hands or they might get more than they bargained for.

● White hands

Pale, white hands show a yearning for beautiful things but also indicate a certain lack of stamina.

● Pudgy hands

Soft, fat hands with chubby bases to the fingers belong to people with strong sexual appetites. They can be very lazy in other areas of their lives.

20

- **Narrow hands**

Hands which are very narrow show a cold nature, particularly if the palm is hollow.

- **Thin hands**

Thin hands reflect a reserved personality. People with thin hands are afraid to show their feelings. They need to be nurtured in a relationship but respond well to warmth.

- **Cold hands**

Cold hands denote a circulation problem but also a warm heart.

- **Clammy hands**

These are not very pleasant to shake. Clammy hands reveal a nervous character, the sort of person who wants to achieve things in life but somehow can't get round to it.

The nails

- **Pink nails**

A healthy individual with a good level of energy.

- **Red nails**

A very hot-blooded nature.

- **White nails**

Reveal a vitamin or mineral deficiency and a supplement is advisable.

- **Bitten nails**

These are the sign of the nervous, frustrated individual who finds too many obstacles in his or her path.

● Large nails

In some cases these are also long but it is not essential. These belong to born leaders. They are strong, loyal and slow to anger but watch out when they lose their temper.

● Short nails

A critical nature, practical, argumentative but brave.

● Oval nails

These are very attractive to look at and indicate a sensitive, intuitive type. Idealistic, the owner of oval nails is often disappointed when life doesn't live up to his or her expectations.

● Round nails

These are usually found on hot-tempered, sexy characters. Though they are inclined to be jealous they never bear malice after an argument.

● Square nails

These are unmistakable and the sign of an outspoken rather tactless character. However, the subject with square nails is also likely to be honest, straightforward and hard-working and worth getting to know despite his or her brutally frank tongue.

Hair on the back of the hand

Most men have hair on the back of their hands. If it is fair and fine and seems to 'match' the hand itself, then the owner will be refined and sophisticated in his tastes. Thick hair, particularly if it is dark suggests an ardent, sensuous nature.

The proportions

Look at the hand, palm uppermost. If the distance from the base of the palm to the base of the fingers is noticeably greater than the distance from the base of the fingers to their tips, the subject is likely to have a highly sensuous nature and sex is frequently on his or her mind. In extreme cases where the difference in size is very great and the hand also has a heavy thumb, the subject could be cruel and even violent.

Should the fingers be noticeably longer than the palm their owner is likely to be more interested in mental pursuits than physical and is also inclined to be critical. Ideally palm and fingers should be of even size showing a happy balance between the physical and mental aspects of his or her nature.

The basic hand shapes

Once you've learned all you can from the overall appearance of the hand the next step is to consider its shape. Palmists usually divide hands into four basic shapes: spatulate, conical, square and pointed.

It's quite possible to see a hand which combines characteristics from two or even three of the basic shapes and in these cases we refer to them as mixed hands. Mixed hands have their own meaning but it's also a good idea to look up the meanings of the other shapes present as well since the owner is likely to be a real mixed personality.

The spatulate hand

The spatulate hand has a large, broad palm with thick, blunt fingers widening at the tips to resemble a spatula. The palm is often hard and unyielding rather than springy in texture.

23

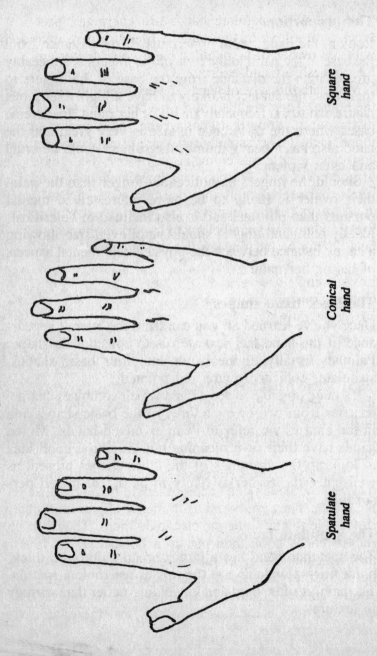

Square
hand

Conical
hand

Spatulate
hand

People with spatulate hands are energetic, practical types with a love of the outdoor life. If you're involved with the owner of a spatulate hand you'd better enjoy a lot of fresh air and exercise.

Men with this type of hand are very useful to have about the house. They are natural do-it-yourselfers and can fix just about anything that goes wrong. They prefer action to intellectual discussion but they are usually good fathers and make gentle but enthusiastic lovers. They have lot of stamina in bed. Women with spatulate hands share the same characteristics as the men and are likely to excel at cookery. On the negative side, seen in extreme forms the spatulate hand can belong to a workaholic who channels all his or her energy into their career.

Love rating: ★ ★ ★ ★ ★
Companionship rating: ★ ★ ★
Marriage rating: ★ ★ ★ ★

Conical

The conical hand has a long palm which tapers towards the top. The fingers are full at the base and slightly pointed at the tip with long nails. The owners of conical hands like art, beautiful things, good food and stimulating conversation.

They can be good companions and are well suited to marriage, although don't expect them to be practical about the house. They are bored by domestic chores and prefer if possible to pay someone else to do them. They'd much rather read a book than put up a bookshelf. As lovers they lack the energy of the more robust spatulate hands but what they lack in stamina they make up in imagination. On the negative side, they can be moody and emotional and if the fingertips are hard the owner can be argumentative.

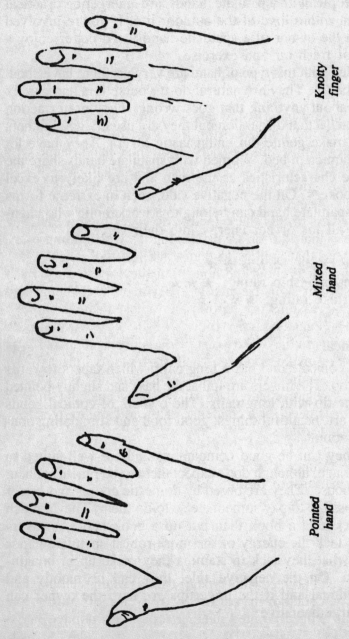

Knotty
finger

Mixed
hand

Pointed
hand

Love rating: ★ ★ ★
Companionship: ★ ★ ★ ★
Marriage: ★ ★ ★ ★

Square

The square hand is the most common shape of all. The palm forms a square from the wrist to the base of the fingers. Since this is such a common hand shape it is necessary to examine the fingers for a more accurate interpretation but, in general, the square hand is a very capable hand.

Owners of this shape tend to do everything well. They believe that if a job's worth doing it's worth doing properly and that applies to their love life too. These types are practical about the house but they're often too busy to use their skills frequently. They adore a challenge and for this reason work hard in their chosen career but they also appreciate family life.

As lovers they take great pains to please their partners and they make good marriage partners as long as their spouse continues to be a challenge and not a doormat. On the negative side, they can be changeable and difficult and their need for a challenge can lead them to overwork and into affairs.

Love rating: ★ ★ ★ ★
Companionship rating: ★ ★ ★
Marriage: ★ ★ ★

Pointed

Long and pointed, this type of hand is often seen in paintings but seldom in real life. It is even more rare to see a man with a pointed hand. People with pointed hands are likely to be very psychic with a fascination for the occult. They tend to get strong hunches and premonitions and can 'see through' people easily.

They are inclined to be fastidious and pernickety, they can't rest if there's a speck of dust or a book out of place. Nevertheless they often have a good sense of humour and a quick wit and make entertaining companions. Despite this they're not very interested in sex and frequently prefer to live alone. On the negative side they can be obsessive about hygiene and too 'cranky' to get on with.

Love rating: ★
Companionship rating: ★ ★ ★
Marriage rating: ★

Mixed

Sometimes a hand does not fit into any of these categories but contains elements of all four. These are known as mixed hands and the owners are often clever adaptable types who can get on with anyone they choose.

They have ingenious, analytical minds and move from interest to interest delving deeply into each subject before moving on. They are unlikely to stray and often have long and happy marriages providing their spouses don't demand their undivided attention all the time. They make enthusiastic lovers when they put their minds to it. On the negative side, they can be boring if you don't share their fascination for their latest interest and taken to extremes these types can become so preoccupied they have no time for anything or anyone else.

Love rating: ★ ★
Companionship: ★ ★
Marriage: ★ ★ ★

The fingers

Having decided on the general shape of the hand the next thing to do is consider the fingers. First, look at all four fingers together. Are they long or short? Generally speaking, short fingers indicate impulsive, quick thinking characters. On the positive side they can be wonderful, stimulating companions, but in a negative hand they can be irritable and impatient.

Long fingers show a more reflective temperament. People with long fingers consider a problem from every angle before committing themselves. They are patient and analytical and take endless trouble over tiny details. At their best, they make thoughtful and considerate partners. At their worst they can be critical of others and maddeningly slow.

Should the base of the fingers be thick and fleshy the subject is highly sensuous with a powerful sex drive. If the base of the fingers is thin, their owner is more interested in mental pursuits than physical pleasures. When the line formed, where the base of the fingers joins the palm, slopes steeply downhill towards the little finger, the subject is likely to have been born in comparatively humble circumstances. He or she will only achieve the good things in life through hard work. Should all four fingers be set in a straight line − a more unusual sight − their owner is likely to have inherited wealth or been brought up in a rich family.

The individual fingers

Over the years palmistry has been linked with astrology and probably for this reason, the fingers and some of the mounts (the fleshy pads on the palm of the hand) are named after the planets. The first finger, or index finger, is known as Jupiter. The second finger, Saturn. The third finger or ring finger is called Apollo and the fourth or little finger is Mercury. The length of each finger tells

29

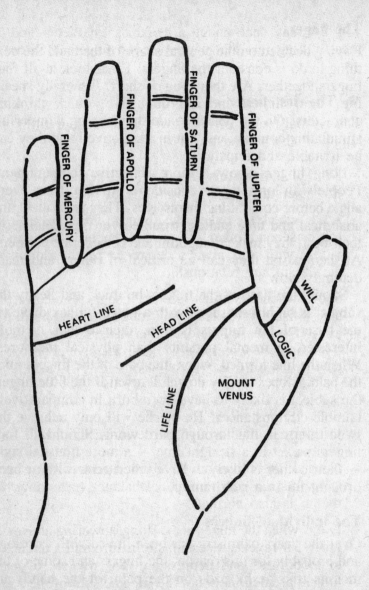

FINGER OF MERCURY

FINGER OF APOLLO

FINGER OF SATURN

FINGER OF JUPITER

WILL

HEART LINE

HEAD LINE

LOGIC

LIFE LINE

MOUNT
VENUS

you a great deal about a person's character and is
measured against that of the second finger of Saturn.

● The first finger of Jupiter
The normal length of this finger is about four-fifths the
length of the second finger of Saturn.

— Normal length: this shows a level-headed, down to
earth person who is considerate of others.

— Long: when this finger is as long as, or almost as long
as, the second finger of Saturn it denotes a bossy individual who will always desire to be the dominant
partner in any relationship.

— Short: when this finger is short it suggests a cowardly
and selfish nature. The owner of such a finger will put
himself or herself before others every time. Should
this finger be excessively short, the owner probably
suffers from an inferiority complex.

● The second finger of Saturn
In the normal hand Saturn is the longest finger.

— Normal: this shows a well adjusted person who is able
to maintain a good emotional balance (providing the
thumb is also normal).

— Long: when the finger is overlong, towering above the
others, it reveals a pessimistic nature and a tendency
to moodiness and depression. The owners of such
fingers are definitely not the life and soul of the party
types.

— Short: this indicates a flighty, immature character who
may never be ready to settle down to the responsibility

of a family. These Peter Pan types think only of pleasure and the moment.

● **The third finger of Apollo**

The normal length of the third finger of Apollo or ring finger, is roughly nine-tenths that of the second finger of Saturn.

 — Normal: a normal Apollo finger shows a healthy appreciation of art and beauty as well as the physical things in life.

 — Long: this reveals an intellectual and ambitious outlook. The owner of such a finger is inclined to take a calculated risk. Should the finger be excessively long, watch out — the subject could be a compulsive gambler.

 — Short: this indicates a rather philistine nature. The owner of the short finger of Apollo is not interested in art, neither is he or she an intellectual.

● **The fourth finger of Mercury**

The normal length of the fourth finger of Mercury or little finger is about seven-tenths the length of the second finger of Saturn. If this finger is thick it shows an argumentative nature, particularly if the thumb is also stiff (see next section). When this finger is thin it is associated with a love of music. It can also hint at psychic powers.

 — Normal: this shows a gregarious, adaptable personality. The sort of person who gets on easily with others.

 — Long: sometimes this finger is almost as long as the third finger of Apollo. This denotes an articulate person, possibly even an outstanding orator to whom tact and diplomacy are second nature. This person will never have trouble putting his or her feelings into words.

↙ Short: a hasty nature and an acid tongue.

● **The thumb**

When considering the fingers it's important to bear in mind that their influences can be overridden or nullified altogether by the thumb. The thumb is the most important digit on the hand. It is the symbol of self, of will and of intellect.

A poor or 'weak' thumb can 'dilute' the beneficial influences of the most perfect fingers, while a strong thumb can counteract the bad effect of less than ideal fingers. A strong thumb accompanying straight, even, well balanced fingers is the ideal, indicating an honest, intelligent, good natured disposition with enough willpower and discipline to put plans into action.

When the thumb is held close to the first finger of Jupiter it usually reaches the first joint, or just below it. A thumb which reaches above the joint is known as a long thumb, well below it, it is classed as short. Our distant relatives the chimpanzees are equipped with rudimentary thumbs (as well as some of the major lines on the palm) and these are short and set very low down on their hands. Occasionally you see a man with just such a primitive thumb and this indicates a lack of intellect.

Generally a long thumb belongs to someone whose head rules his or her heart, a short thumb to someone who is too soft for his or her own good. These people get walked all over. Owners of the normal or average thumb fall somewhere between the two. They are not pushovers for sob stories but you certainly couldn't call them hard hearted.

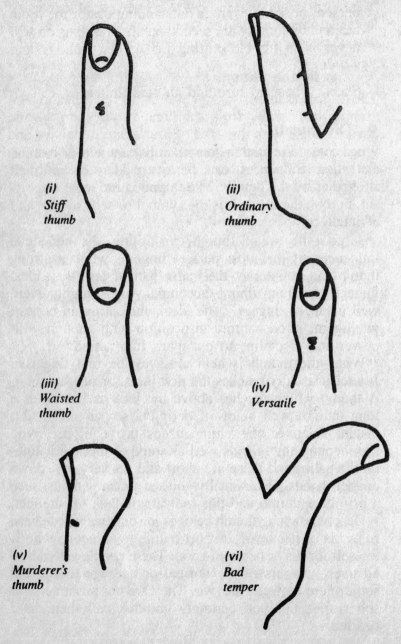

(i)
*Stiff
thumb*

(ii)
*Ordinary
thumb*

(iii)
*Waisted
thumb*

(iv)
Versatile

(v)
*Murderer's
thumb*

(vi)
*Bad
temper*

Palmists divide thumbs into two types, the flexible and the inflexible thumb. This might sound strange at first but when you look closely, the difference is obvious.

● The flexible thumb

The flexible thumb is springy and distinctive, the top joint arching back away from the hand in an unmistakable curve. People with this type of thumb are impulsive and gregarious. The sort who would like to whisk away to Paris at a moment's notice. Their natures are as flexible as their thumbs. They are broad minded and enjoy change.

● The inflexible thumb

The inflexible thumb is straight and firm and rather stiff when pushed back. The owners of this type of thumb are rather more set in their ways. Once they've made up their minds they stick to them. They are reliable and hard-working and unlikely to take risks especially where money is concerned.

As well as dividing the thumb into two main types, palmists also examine the two joints, or phalanges, separately.

The first phalange
The first, or top, phalange shows the degree of will-power and determination. If this phalange looks rather wide giving the thumb a slightly top heavy appearance, the subject is likely to have so much determination to get his or her own way that he or she can be stubborn to the point of mulishness. When this appearance is more marked it indicates a quick temper. If the first phalange is thin and weak looking it suggests a timid personality who gives in easily to others.

The second phalange

The second, lower, phalange shows the degree of intelligence and reasoning powers. Ideally both phalanges should be of equal length, indicating a balance between logic and will-power. When the second phalange is longer than the first it is the sign of a person who reasons everything very carefully before acting.

Sometimes this joint has a waisted appearance. There is nothing wrong with this. It shows a tactful tongue allied to a logical brain. But when the thumb looks excessively waisted you are dealing with a cunning individual who might well deceive.

● The murderer's thumb

This sounds rather alarming and thankfully such thumbs are rare. Usually found on men, murderer's thumbs are very short and the first phalange is so over-developed as to appear bulbous. The owner of such a thumb is not necessarily a murderer but you wouldn't want to pick a fight with him. He has a wicked temper, is easily provoked and takes it personally if anyone disagrees with him. This is an explosive combination particularly since such types are usually of low intelligence and find it difficult to express themselves verbally. All too often they resort to violence and sometimes this leads to murder.

I've only seen a few of these thumbs in my years of studying palmistry. I remember one client who came to me in tears because her new husband had arrived home late one night, there was an argument over his spoiled dinner and instead of apologising he'd beaten her. She rolled up her sleeves to show me the blue and yellow bruises breaking out across her arms.

Her husband, it turned out, had a murderer's thumb. I was forced to warn her that I didn't think there was much hope for their marriage. Although he might be sorry afterwards, her husband was bound to attack her again. When he got angry he couldn't help himself and such men are notoriously easy to annoy. The poor girl didn't want to believe it, of course. She persuaded herself that the incident was a freak brainstorm and would never happen again. She went back to her husband. It was only after she'd landed up in hospital a couple of times that she realised I was right. The last I heard of her she was staying at a refuge for battered wives.

CHAPTER THREE:
THE LOVE LINES

Open your hand and look at the palm. The first thing that
will strike you is that three major lines stand out from
the rest. Some palms are smooth, others are covered in
a maze of tiny marks like little hairs, but no matter what
type of palm you have, the major lines will dominate it.

Starting beneath the fingers, the first line you come to
is called the **Heart line**. This begins at the outer edge
of the palm, and makes its way across to end beneath
the fingers. The next line down is called the **Head line**.
The head line starts near the opposite edge of the palm
and moves towards the centre of the hand. The line below
this which curves round the base of the thumb is called
the **Life line**. The fleshy area encircled by the life line
is known as the **Mount of Venus**.

Apart from a few rare individuals who have a combined heart and head line which runs across the palm in
a single unbroken line (more about that later) we all have
these three major lines, yet the different shapes, lengths,
branches off and configurations of these lines is endless.
It really is true to say that no two hands are the same.
If there is anyone close by as you read this, glance at
their hands and you will see immediately that the three
major lines are quite different from your own.

All these lines have their own complex meanings and,
of course, there are many other lesser lines on the palm
worthy of study, but as far as love is concerned there

are three areas I think of as the love lines: the heart line, the mount of Venus and another line which does not even count as a major line but is important in affairs of the heart nevertheless, the girdle of Venus (see diagram).

Incidentally, when you are examining the love lines be sure to look at both hands. Basically, if the subject is right-handed his left hand shows the characteristics he was born with and his right hand shows what he has done with them and how he has developed over the years. The opposite applies to a left-handed subject.

The Heart line

Charlotte was a very attractive young woman. She had long blonde hair, huge brown eyes and a slim, lithe figure. She was the sort of woman who turned heads wherever she went, yet despite all her obvious assets she was convinced that her husband was having an affair.

'When we're out I catch him looking at other girls,' she said, 'and for the last three months he's been working late at the office practically every night. I'm sure he's got someone else.'

Now of course a lot of sudden and unusual overtime can sometimes mean that the person concerned is misbehaving. But it can also mean that they are working hard to earn extra cash or to advance themselves in their career. I also had to point out to Charlotte that glancing at other women proved nothing more than the fact that her husband was a normal healthy male. Before she upset an otherwise happy marriage, Charlotte needed a lot more to go on and intuitively I felt that her husband wasn't at fault.

When I looked at Charlotte's palm this feeling grew stronger. There was no sign of a break-up in her hand. Nevertheless her heart line swept across her palm in a wide curve, swinging up to rest tightly between the first

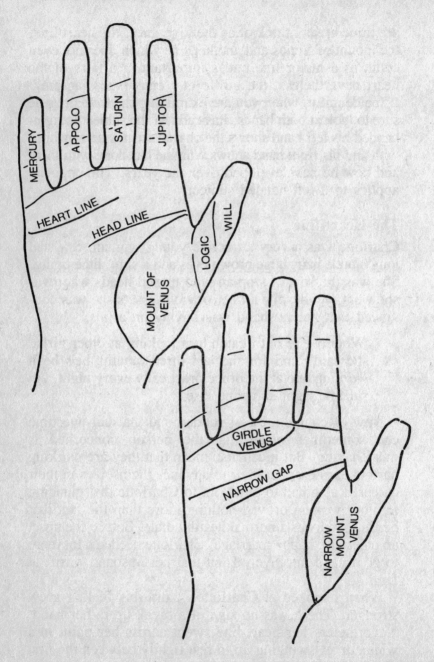

finger of Jupiter and the second finger of Saturn, right on the webbing that separated the two fingers. I was looking at the classic jealous heart line.

> 'Of course I can't be sure without seeing your husband's hand,' I said to Charlotte, 'but I feel that you've got nothing to worry about. You're inclined to be possessive and that's what's making you think like this.'

Charlotte later sent me copies of her husband's hands and I saw that I was right. He was an honest, loyal man who thought the world of her. There was no sign of unfaithfulness at all. I was able to explain to Charlotte that her fears were groundless at the moment but she must be careful. If she didn't control her jealous nature she might end up driving her husband into the arms of another woman.

It's extraordinary that one line can tell you so much, but when it comes to love, the heart line is the most important line on the hand. The colouring, shape, length and ending of this line can give a wonderfully accurate picture of a person's emotional make-up.

The combinations are endless, of course, but here I've only got space for the more usual types.

● Appearance

Ideally the heart line should be deep, clear and pink, showing a normal, well balanced person in whom the emotions and physical appetites are in harmony. A deep red line betrays a passionate nature, so passionate that it's unlikely the subject will be satisfied with one partner. Should this line be very dark and wide it hints at a tendency towards violence. A thin, pale line indicates poor stamina in bed and if this line is so thin it looks like a thread, the owner will be an indifferent and selfish lover.

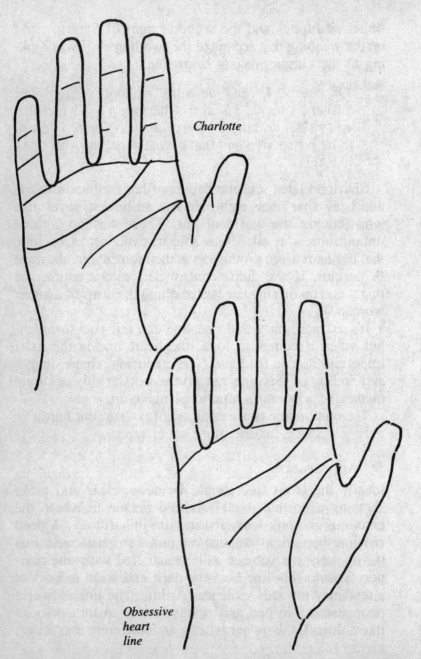

Charlotte

*Obsessive
heart
line*

● **Position**

When the heart line starts low in the hand (some can start almost half-way down the palm) the owner is cautious and slow to make a move. They will wait for their partner to declare love before revealing their own true feelings. When the heart line is very high, springing across just beneath the fingers, it suggests a passionate, impulsive person who falls in love easily and is not inhibited about showing it.

As you might expect the line that begins midway between these extremes reflects a nature that is also balanced between the two.

● **Types**

There are many, many different heart lines but the ones I've seen over the years have mainly fallen into two basic groups: the single heart line and the branched line.

Generally speaking, the single heart line belongs to the sort of person who is straightforward emotionally, while the heart line which ends in two or more branches shows a more complicated character. The more branches the more complex the individual's love life is likely to be. In fact, I've seen heart lines which fan out into five or six lines at the end so that they resemble a brush. In cases like these I'd suggest the subject should not settle down too early in life because he finds it difficult to make up his mind and he needs a lot of variety.

Once again, in general the straighter the heart line, the less emotional the owner is likely to be in love. A dead straight line would indicate the type of person who puts business before pleasure every time. The more the heart line curves up towards the fingers, the more emotional and jealous the subject is likely to be. The length of line is important too. Basically, the longer the line the warmer the feelings. A very short heart line reaching only as far as the fourth finger of Apollo suggests a cold nature.

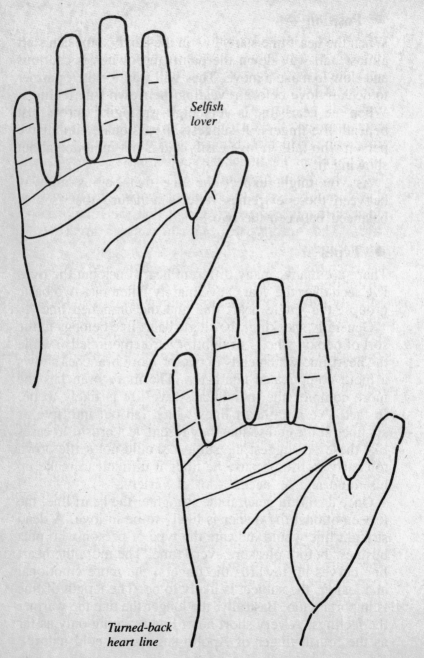

Selfish
lover

Turned-back
heart line

● The endings

The place where the heart line comes to an end is particularly significant. A heart line which rests on the mount of Jupiter (the fleshy pad beneath the first finger of Jupiter) shows a loyal, loving character. If the line tilts slightly upwards towards the finger it suggests an idealistic temperament, the sort of person who needs to put their lover on a pedestal. Should the line travel up to touch or even climb the finger the subject must be very careful. Their hero-worship tendencies can become obsessive. I've seen this sign in the hands of people who hound their former lovers and never accept that the relationship is over. This unfortunate trait can cause a great deal of unhappiness.

When the heart line ends between the first two fingers of Jupiter and Saturn it shows a jealous nature. If it falls slightly short it reveals less jealousy but an added sentimental streak. The heart line that ends beneath the second finger of Saturn without turning up towards it belongs to a person who is ruled by physical attraction rather than idealistic love and who is likely to be rather selfish in bed.

The line that ends under the fourth finger of Apollo is a sign of a cool, passionless nature. Occasionally, you see a heart line which curls back on itself towards the little finger of Mercury. This shows that an emotional relationship will be connected to money in some way. I've seen this sort of line in the hands of girls who marry much older, richer men.

Sometimes the heart line reaches the mount of Saturn (the fleshy pad beneath the second finger of Saturn) and then turns down towards the head line. This indicates a person whose head rules his heart. These types are cool, undemonstrative and hard to please. Just the opposite are those people whose heart line divides into two on the mount of Jupiter. They are idealistic, affectionate and

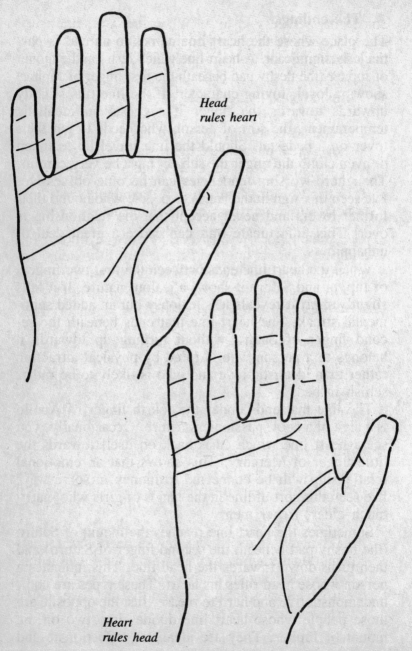

*Head
rules heart*

*Heart
rules head*

sometimes reckless in love. When the heart line starts strongly, then thins out noticeably it's an indication that the affections will wane in later life.

● Unusual heart lines

— The double heart line: this is a lovely sign to have. It shows great physical strength, and the sort of person who is a kind, devoted partner and a good provider.

— The triple heart line: this is extremely rare and indicates love and passion in abundance.

— The simian line: just lately I've seen an increasing number of simian lines, yet at one time they were very unusual. I don't know why this should be but the simian line in which the heart line and head line are joined together to form one line across the palm, suggests a person who has great intensity of purpose and will never settle for second best. I don't think I've ever seen the simian line in both hands but when this occurs it's not such a happy sign for prospective lovers. It indicates a person who will channel all that intensity into their career. These types are too busy for love.

● Marks on the heart line

As well as indicating the sort of love that best suits you and your prospective partner the heart line can also fortell events ahead.

— Breaks in the line: a break in the heart line reveals an emotional trauma, probably a broken relationship. Often a sister line appears close to the break to mend the troubled spot. This is a sign that the lover could return to heal the rift.

— Upward lines: lines going up from the heart line show

47

that the relationship is happy and stable, although a great many fine lines hint at flirtations.

— Downward lines: lines falling down from the heart line show disappointments in love.

— Chained: when the heart line appears to be composed entirely of 'bubbles' all linked together, this is known as a chained heart line. It's not a promising sign and indicates a fickle, unfaithful lover.

— Cross: a cross on the heart line warns that financial problems could be the cause of a marital breakdown.

— Circle: this is an unusual configuration to find on a hand but is sometimes seen and suggests a possible separation.

— Triangle: this is a very lucky sign. The bearer of a triangle on the heart line will always be lucky in love.

— Square: a square will often form around an adverse mark, such as a break. This shows protection from whatever harm is threatened. In the case of a break on the heart line this could mean that a separation is likely but averted at the last minute by positive action — perhaps the partners seek outside counselling.

— Grilles: wherever you find them, grilles are not a happy sign. They mean stress and worry ahead but they do fade away when the problems are over.

The mount of Venus

Although the heart line is the most important love line, the mount of Venus, encircled by the life line, must never be overlooked. Basically the fuller the curve of the life line, the larger the mount and the more loving, affectionate and sympathetic the subject will be. People with well developed mounts of Venus always have time for those less fortunate than themselves and they are generous in every way, with their time, money and affection.

The shallower the curve, the more cautious and reserved the character. These people are not mean but they are careful in all things and unlikely to be taken in by hard luck stories. Should the life line hug the base of the thumb and fall down the palm in a straight line it shows a miserly, suspicious nature. These people are not life's givers and that applies to their affections too.

In general the fleshier the mount, the more ardent the nature. A flat mount accompanied by a widely curving life line suggests a kind, generous temperament but a person who expresses love in a spiritual rather than physical way. A tireless charity worker, for example, might have this type of hand.

● Marks on the mount of Venus

- Horizontal lines: we'd all like a few horizontal lines on the mount of Venus for these are the sign of a person who is attractive to members of the opposite sex. A great many horizontal lines suggests a flirt.

- Vertical lines: these lines come and go and show drawbacks in a relationship. Every relationship goes through its less blissful moments and that's when these lines appear. They soon fade when minor irritations disappear.

- Influence lines: sometimes you see a deep line which starts within the mount of Venus, crosses the life line and goes straight across the hand to the marriage lines (see the Marriage M). Sometimes this line is also feathered in appearance. It means that a person who is already attached to someone else, is going to have a great impact on your life and marriage. This person is not necessarily a lover. It could be a member of the family. They might influence you in some way or they could even come to live with you.

49

I recently saw this mark in the hand of a woman who was agonising over whether she should provide a home for her elderly mother. She wasn't happy about the situation but she was a kind-hearted lady and her conscience dictated that she should act. Space was short in the household but she moved her mother into the family home. This did mean that the marriage was put under more strain but if she had hardened her heart she would have suffered so much guilt that it would have caused rows with her husband anyway.

The girdle of Venus

The girdle of Venus is a semi-circular line which is found beneath the fingers but above the heart line. The line can be full, broken into small pieces or completely non-existent. Its presence or absence give an indication of the subject's sexual appetite.

— Full girdle: this shows an ardent individual whose passions are very close to the surface.

— Broken girdle: when the girdle is fragmented in this way it indicates a hot-blooded nature but one that is more controlled than the case above.

— No girdle: the absence of a girdle of Venus does not necessarily mean that the subject is lacking in passion, simply that he keeps his feelings under control until he is sure the time is right.

A lot of lines under the girdle, particularly if accompanied by a little hook on the heart line, show a taste for kinky sex. A grille inside the girdle of Venus means that sexual intrigue could injure a career. I would imagine a lot of politicians who find themselves involved in scandal would have this sign. They would do well to check their hands first before embarking on a potentially embarrassing affair.

CHAPTER FOUR:
SHOULD YOU GET INVOLVED?

Not long ago I was having coffee with a few women friends. The conversation turned to family celebrations and one of the women, I'll call her Anne to spare her embarrassment, mentioned that her wedding anniversary was looming up. Now since this woman rarely had a good word to say for her husband I gathered that she wouldn't be doing much celebrating when the occasion arrived.

'Too right I won't,' she said rather bitterly. 'If I'd known then what I know now I'd never have married him.'

Sadly, she meant it. The couple were only staying together for convenience. Although their children were long since grown they'd decided that the upheaval of divorce and the expense of two households simply wasn't worth the bother. They might as well continue to lead separate lives under one roof.

'If only I'd said goodbye at the end of that first evening and refused to see him again,' said Anne, 'how different my life might have been.'

In actual fact I believe it's never too late to start again, but that's beside the point. I didn't want to make Anne's sufferings any worse by pointing out that she could have discovered the clues to her husband's future behaviour, simply by looking at his palm on that very first date. Had she been able to read the signs I'm sure she would have had nothing more to do with him.

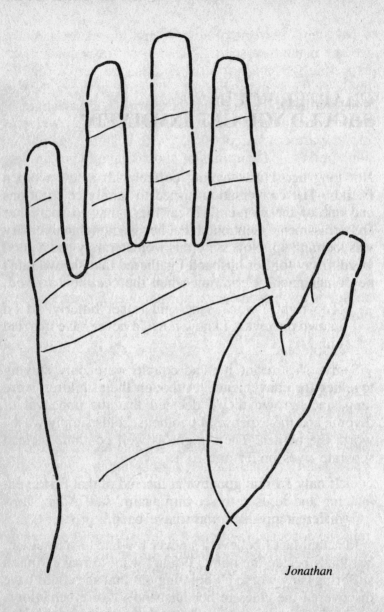

Jonathan

52

No one is perfect, of course, and too many men and women make themselves and their partners unhappy by expecting too much from their other halves, forgetting that they themselves aren't exactly without faults. Nevertheless it has to be said that there are certain weaknesses that no one in their right mind would willingly welcome in a partner. Alcoholics, wife-beaters, gamblers, adulterers . . . Thousands of people have to put up with them when the prince or princess they may turns into a frog after the wedding.

That's not to say that such unfortunates are entirely hopeless cases. Many of them struggle against and eventually overcome their problems. But given the choice, most people would prefer to save themselves the heartache of falling in love with so badly flawed an individual. After all, life is troublesome enough without adding unnecessary burdens.

Fortunately, the clues which reveal the worst problems are simple and easy to read in the hand.

The alcoholic

Jonathan was clearly upset when he came to see me. He was a big, strong, healthy looking man with fine brown hair and a warm complexion. He was neatly dressed in good quality clothes and anyone passing him in the street would have marked him down as a particularly fortunate man.

My first impression was that if he had problems they must be concerned with his career. A man like Jonathan would surely have no trouble attracting women. Yet before he'd even sat down Jonathan blurted out that he'd come to me because something had gone wrong with his marriage.

'Well, not so much the marriage I suppose, as me,' he said. 'The other day we had an argument and I

53

hit my wife. I can't understand it. I'm not a violent person. I've never laid a finger on her in anger in five years of marriage but the other night. . . I couldn't seem to help myself.'

I glanced quickly at Jonathan's thumb. It was not a classic violent thumb at all. Just the opposite, if anything.

'Well, let's have a look at your hands,' I said.

The moment he turned his palms over I could see what was wrong. He had the classic sign of the alcoholic. A strong, deep line went from the mount of Venus inside the life line and marched its way right across to the outer side of his hand. Worse still, there was an identical line in both hands. There was no doubt that Jonathan was an alcoholic.

'Tell me,' I said, 'had you been drinking when you had that row?'

Jonathan looked a bit shifty.

'Well, yes. But only a couple of beers. I wasn't drunk if that's what you mean,' he said indignantly.

I had to break it to him that I believed he had a serious problem.

'If you don't get help as soon as possible,' I said, 'you risk losing your wife.'

Naturally, Jonathan wasn't exactly delighted with this interpretation but he eventually agreed that lately his drinking had been getting out of hand. He would think about giving it up, he promised. I didn't want to say anything to jeopardise his chances but frankly I didn't think he'd be able to cope. The top joint of his thumb was small and weak looking, suggesting that he had very little will-power. Had that joint been well developed and strong he would have had the self discipline to overcome his problem. As it was I didn't hold out much hope for him. Sadly I heard some months later that Jonathan's wife had left him, he'd lost his job and if he wasn't careful he'd end up losing his home as well.

The suicidal type

I've never met Amanda but she has been writing to me for several years now and her story is one that I will never forget. She first got in touch after reading about my work in a magazine article. She was very interested to hear that I could give readings from photocopied hands and she explained that this would be ideal for her because she lived much too far from London to come for a personal consultation.

She enclosed copies of her own hands and although I don't encourage people to tell me about their lives she wanted me to know a few details because there was a specific question she wanted to ask. She hadn't been very lucky in love in the past, but she'd recently met a man to whom she seemed well suited. They shared a number of interests, he was kind and considerate and he often stayed at Amanda's home where he seemed very happy. Best of all he'd proposed and Amanda was much inclined to say yes but she was a little wary. She had been hurt several times in the past and she'd only known her new lover a few months. Did I think he was the man for her?

Now, of course, it was very difficult for me to say without seeing the young man's hands but I could tell at a glance that Amanda had problems ahead and those problems concerned her love life. There was a series of stress grilles – little networks of criss cross lines – around her heart line near the centre of her palm. This told me that there was heartache and strain in the near future.

Since this timing coincided with the date of her proposed wedding I could only conclude that there would

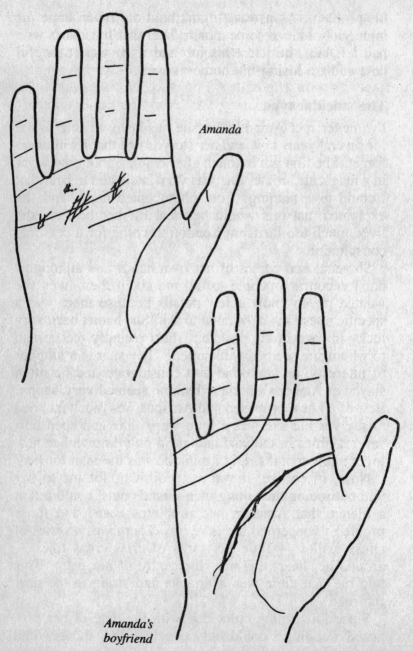

Amanda

*Amanda's
boyfriend*

be quite severe marriage problems. I didn't feel it would be at all wise to go ahead with the wedding but before putting a damper on Amanda's spirits I advised her to do nothing hasty but to send me copies of her boyfriend's hands as soon as possible. I don't know what excuse she gave but Amanda managed to obtain the copies and forwarded them to me practically by return of post.

The hands, as I'd feared, showed a very sad case. The man's head line, instead of running across his hand, turned sharply downwards and veered steeply towards his wrist, indicating not just depression but suicidal tendencies. As well as this, his heart line climbed up towards the second finger of Saturn, the line even crossing on to the phalange of the finger. This showed a nature that was melancholy in the extreme. Looking at that hand I really felt there was no hope.

This was a case where I felt it would be cruel to mince my words. I told Amanda quite plainly that I did not feel she should marry her boyfriend because he was a potential suicide. There was no reply to my letter. I supposed that she must be offended.

Then six months later, out of the blue, Amanda contacted me again. She had ignored my advice, she explained, probably because it seemed so unlikely and also because every woman believes that she has the power to make her man happy. If her boyfriend got depressed, Amanda felt certain she could cheer him up.

'How wrong I was. I wish now that I'd listened to you,' she wrote.

Apparently three months after the wedding, Amanda's husband had taken an overdose. She came home from work one day and found him dead. It was a terrible, terrible shock. Now she was eaten up with guilt. Surely she must have done something to drive him to despair. I found the man's hand prints in my file and looked at them again.

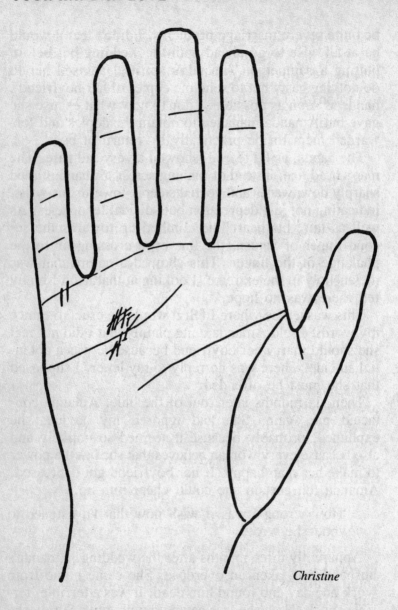

Christine

You could see quite plainly, a zig-zag line crossing the head line as it plummeted down the palm. This showed that he had attempted to take his life before.

'Don't feel bad. It was nothing to do with you,' I told Amanda. 'Your husband has tried this before. Contact his relatives and find out about his background.'

Amanda did as I suggested. She discovered that her husband had survived three previous suicide attempts. The tragic fact was that it was his own personality, not the circumstances of his life, that led him to his final desperate act. He would have killed himself one day whether married or not. Amanda sold her house and moved right away from the district. In time the signs of happiness returned to her hands and she is now peacefully settled with someone else.

The gambler

People often think that it's only women who consult palmists but in truth a great many of my clients are men. Oddly enough, one of them, a man named Gerry, came to see me about a problem he was having with his wife, which turned out to be a weakness which is more commonly found in husbands.

Gerry was at great pains to tell me he was happily married and that he loved his wife but recently things had gone downhill. The couple were quarrelling about money. Suddenly, despite Gerry's well paid job, his wife Christine couldn't manage on the housekeeping any more and they were running into debt. The obvious answer seemed to be that Christine must be buying all sorts of things she couldn't afford, yet Gerry insisted his wife had bought nothing new for months.

Gerry's hands were square, his fingers straight and well proportioned and his mount of Venus was full. He was clearly an honest, loyal, considerate man. Often in marital disputes, it's a case of six of one and half a dozen of the other, but this I felt was a situation where the problem must lie with his wife. I asked if Gerry could persuade Christine to come and see me. He was worried at first because he didn't want her to find out that he'd been himself.

'She'd think it was disloyal of me discussing our problems with someone else,' he said.

But then he hit on the perfect solution. Christine's birthday fell in a few weeks' time.

'She loves all this sort of thing,' he said, 'I'll give her a reading as a birthday present.'

As it turned out Christine was thrilled with what she considered to be a most imaginative if rather unusual gift. She came along happily. When I looked at her hands I saw that she was well suited to her husband. There was only one weak area. Her third finger of Apollo was overlong and heavier than the other fingers. And when she held her hand relaxed, there were wide gaps between the fingers. That over-developed Apollo finger told me that she was a gambler at heart and the spaces between her fingers showed that she was hopeless with money. It slipped through her hands like water.

'Tell me Christine, do you ever gamble?' I asked. 'Oh no,' she said, horrified, 'I only go to bingo.'

Christine, like so many people, thought of gambling in terms of casinos or betting shops and it wouldn't have crossed her mind to enter either. She'd never even thought of going to a bingo session until a woman at work took her along to one on a night when Gerry was doing overtime. Immediately Christine was hooked. She loved it and she'd fallen into the habit of going three or four times a week, never daring to tell her husband how much money she was spending. I advised her that there were problems ahead concerned with money and she should cut down, or cut out altogether, her bingo sessions. If she didn't she might put her marriage at risk.

'Mmmm. I suppose you're right,' said Christine reluctantly. Then she changed the subject. 'What about children? Do you see any children for me?'

As it happened I saw two. Then I had a flash of clairvoyance.

'You're not pregnant already, are you?'
'No such luck,' said Christine.

But a few weeks later she phoned me.

'I don't know how you knew,' she laughed, 'but the doctor's just confirmed it. I'm six weeks pregnant!'

Christine was one of the lucky ones. She became so wrapped up in her children that there was no time for bingo. Yet she will always have to be careful. By nature she is a compulsive gambler and at slacker periods in her life she will have to fight the urge to find excitement by risking money.

Christine's story doesn't sound particularly dramatic because her 'vice' was only bingo. Some people lose hundreds of thousands in one night on the roulette wheel. Many of them can afford it but others sell first the yacht, then the car and finally the house as their compulsion drives them further and further into debt. Yet the problem is just the same and those wealthy addicts who squander fortunes will carry the same marks in their hands that Christine bears to this day.

The flirt

This is more commonly a female phenomenon and I saw a good example quite recently when a young, up and

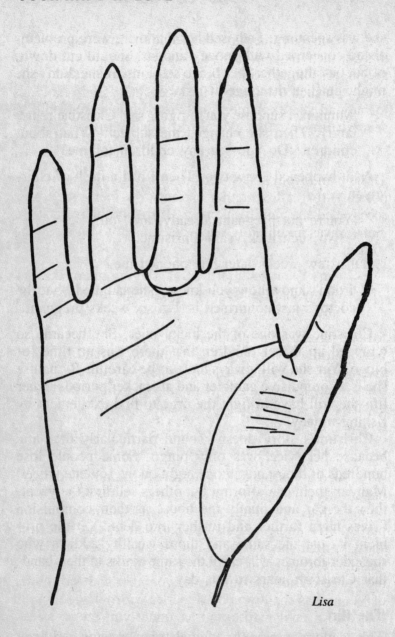

Lisa

coming actress came for a consultation. Lisa was a strikingly attractive girl with wild, red-gold hair, unusual long green eyes and the kind of creamy complexion that often goes with such colouring. Her face was vaguely familiar to me and she explained that she had appeared on TV several times — though only in small parts.

'Blink and you'd miss me!' she laughed.

She came from a show business family too and it was possible that I'd seen her parents on the screen and recognised the family likeness. Lisa's problem, at first glance, was an unlikely one. She wanted to know about romance.

'I can't seem to find a man,' she complained, 'and Mummy and Daddy keep nagging me to get married. I think it's grandchildren they're really after.'

Looking at her I would have thought that Lisa's problem was fighting men off, not difficulty in attracting them, and it didn't take long to establish that her summary hadn't been strictly accurate. In actual fact, Lisa had dozens of boyfriends. Unfortunately she didn't want to settle down with any of them.

'I never seem to meet anyone special,' she explained.

I looked at her hands. They were long and slender and beautifully manicured. In fact, they were the classic pointed shape indicating that Lisa was fastidious and not particularly interested in sex. She had a long head line showing that she was very intelligent but her heart line was short, ending under the second finger of Saturn and the curve of her life line as it wound round the mount of Venus was shallow. For all her charm and good looks, Lisa had a cool nature and an underlying mean streak — a meannesss not only with money but with her affections too.

Yet despite this, dozens of horizontal lines ran across the mount of Venus and there was a clearly marked girdle or ring around the base of her second finger of Saturn. These signs proved that although Lisa wasn't really interested in a long term relationship, she was vain, she needed to be admired and she was a flirt. No wonder she couldn't settle down. I felt that if she attached herself to a young man, simply to please her parents, she would bring him a great deal of unhappiness.

'What d'you think?' asked Lisa as I pondered over the most diplomatic terms in which to couch my findings. 'Will I ever get married?'

At least here I could give a positive answer. There was one, clear marriage line showing high up in her hand, a sign that she would eventually marry late in life.

'Yes you will,' I told her, 'but not for years yet.'

I went on to explain that really she wasn't ready to settle down yet. She was an independent type, as shown by her head line being separated from her life line at the beginning and her career was more important to her at the moment than an in-depth relationship.

'Play the field and concentrate on your acting,' I advised.

In her heart of hearts Lisa knew I was right and she decided to follow my advice, mainly I suspect because it was what she wanted to do anyway. She could now tell her parents with a clear conscience that her way of life was absolutely right for her and it would be wrong to change it. The last I heard she was packing her bags to try her luck in Hollywood.

The womaniser

It may sound sexist to say this but the male equivalent
of the flirt is usually the womaniser. Far from having an
excess of loving feelings this sort of man is often cold
and selfish. I met Tony at a party. Like many people he
was incredulous but also fascinated when he discovered
that I'm a palmist. He asked me lots of questions and
talked for so long that I began to realise his interest was
more than just idle curiosity. Sure enough he finally raised
the subject that was uppermost in his mind.

> 'I'm having a few problems at the moment,' he said.
> 'Could you tell me if you see anything about the
> future in my hand?'

When he opened his palm I saw that criss cross stress
lines had traced themselves right across his head line.
Tony's problems were obviously logical and not
emotional. Yet there were dozens of tiny lines around
his marriage line, some faded, some just starting, which
spoke of a great many relationships in the past and the
future.

It turned out that Tony had met another woman and
he wanted to leave his wife for her. The fact that he had
three small children and that his wife would be devastated
didn't bother him unduly. It was the financial implica-
tions of running two households that caused his anxiety.

Tony insisted that his marriage had been a mistake and
that he had now found the right girl for him but looking
at his hand, I wasn't so sure. His heart line started low
down on his palm and went straight to the second finger
of Saturn with many lines coming off it and shooting up
towards the fingers. This is a sure sign of a man who
can't resist variety. In addition the mount of Venus was
weak and the curve shallow, showing a cold and selfish
personality. It was quite obvious that Tony was a
womaniser and that he would not stay with one woman

65

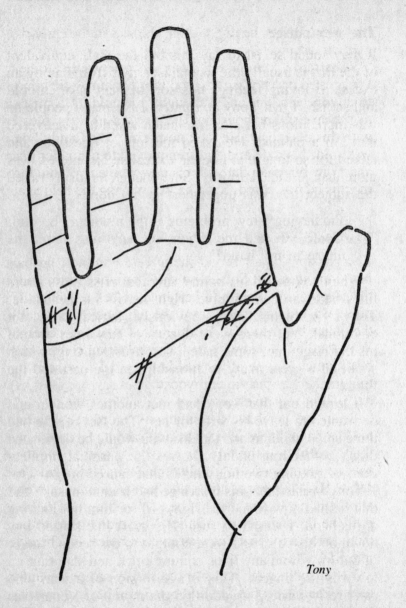

Tony

however 'perfect' he might think she was in the early days of their affair.

I'm afraid I couldn't tell Tony what he wanted to hear. I suggested that it wasn't a good idea for him to tie himself to anyone just yet and I thought it would be a mistake to set up another household. Tony wasn't very pleased with this diagnosis. He took no notice. The family house was sold, his wife and children moved to a smaller place and Tony bought a flat with his new woman. Within three months he was bored. Soon he was playing the field again.

The violent type

The gossip was all round the street. Pauline's husband had done it again. Somehow she'd provoked him and in the ensuing argument he'd beaten her black and blue. The noise was so bad that one of the neighbours had called the police but, as usual, Pauline refused to press charges. Why Pauline stayed with her husband Brian no one knew but a quick glance at his hands when I'd first seen him told me he was the violent type and best avoided. I'd kept out of his way ever since.

Brian did not have the infamous 'murderer's' thumb, but his hands were almost as unpleasant. His palm was thick and heavy, the skin the texture of leather and there was no springiness or 'give' in the flesh. It was hard and solid. His thumb was short and heavy, mount of Venus almost non-existent and his heart line only just reached past the third finger of Apollo. You didn't need to be a palmist to divine that this was a very unpleasant character indeed.

Yet at some stage he had presumably swept the unfortunate Pauline off her feet and convinced her that marriage to him would be a good idea. It's amazing how the majority of such men are married and many of them stay married for years. Perhaps their wives are too frightened

67

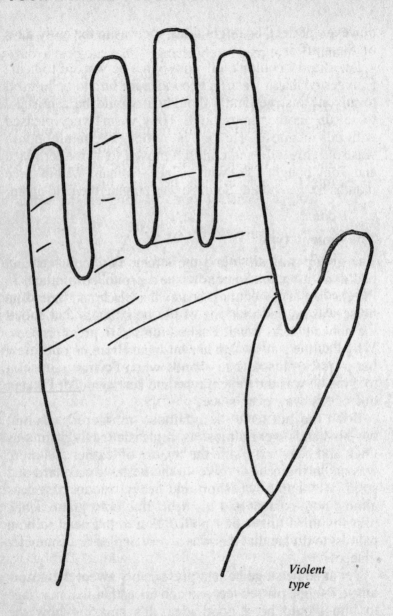

*Violent
type*

to leave. Whatever the reason, it's never a happy situation and violent men rarely change. They are best avoided.

The drug addict

'Bettina,' said one of my regular clients, 'would you do a reading for my daughter? She's eighteen now and doesn't seem to know what she wants to do. You might be able to buck her up a bit.'

'Course I will,' I said, 'as long as she wants to come.'

'Oh I'm sure she'd love it.'

I don't know what young Debbie really thought, but the following week she came along with her mother. She looked rather sullen, almost as if she'd been nagged into the visit, so I decided it would be better if her mother waited outside. Debbie was a thin girl and rather pale but then they often are at that age. She was also highly reserved but that too I dismissed as teenage shyness.

It was only when she showed me her hand that I realised her problems were far more serious. Her palm was dead white, slightly damp and rather limp. Her fingers were weak and narrow, the pads soft and pliable indicating that she was easily led, while her thumb was waisted and insignificant. The child had no will-power. Worse still, a line similar to that of the alcoholic's line ran from inside the mount of Venus across to the edge of her palm. Unlike the alcoholic's line however, this was pale and thin and criss crossed with fret lines. I realised with dismay that I was looking at the hand of a drug addict. Debbie was furious when I asked, very gently, if she'd ever experimented with drugs.

'Oh you're just as bad as my mother!' she yelled.

And with that she jumped up and ran out.

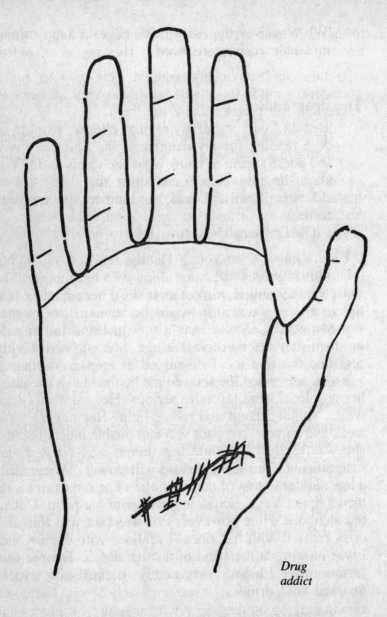

*Drug
addict*

'Whatever's wrong with Debbie?' asked her mother in alarm as the girl raced past.

Debbie had obviously wanted her reading to be confidential but in this case I felt it was vital for her own sake, that her parents knew the truth.

'I'm afraid I've got some rather bad news for you,' I told her mother and I explained what I'd seen.

Today, Debbie is in a clinic where they hope to cure her addiction. By all accounts the treatment is going well, but she'll have a difficult struggle. That weak thumb will make it very hard for her to stick to her resolutions.

The compulsive liar

Gilly sat twisting the engagement ring round and round on her finger. It was a pretty ring. A diamond surrounded by tiny red stones which Gilly believed to be rubies. Unfortunately there was no wedding ring to go with it, and since Gilly was now eight months pregnant this was causing her some distress.

'We were so happy together and he promised. He promised,' she sniffed, on the edge of tears, 'and then someone sent me this.'

She opened her handbag and pulled out a large brown envelope.

'What is it?' I asked.
'Take a look and see.'

I drew out a colour photograph. It was an enlargement of a holiday snap and it showed a typical family holiday in some Mediterranean resort, probably Spain. There was a man playing on the beach with two blond children and beside him lounged an attractive fair haired woman in a bikini. The envelope wasn't quite empty. I shook it and out dropped a scrap of paper. The words 'Did you wonder where your boyfriend was in August?' were scribbled across it in red Biro. It was unsigned.

'This is your fiancé I take it,' I said.

Gilly nodded.

'He told me he was going into hospital in August, something to do with his sinus trouble — and he didn't want any visitors. He made me promise I wouldn't go but he gave me the address of the hospital. I even sent him get well cards . . . And all the time he was in Spain with his family. . . I didn't even know he was married.'

I stared at the picture again. The young man was larking about, his hands held up in front of him in mock horror as he warded off a bucket of sea water. I fetched the magnifying glass I use for such purposes and examined the photograph more closely. There was no doubt about it, Gilly's 'fiancé' had the hand of a liar. His small finger of Mercury was twisted, the classic sign, and it was also long, indicating a convincing and articulate speaker. His head line sloped down into his hand not steeply enough to make him a depressive but it showed that he had an extremely vivid imagination. His lies were likely to be prize whoppers as Gilly had found out but he was able to tell them so well that everyone believed him.

His thumb was small and weak and allied to that twisted finger and over-active imagination I reckoned that this man could even be a Walter Mitty type, living in his own fantasy world. When I explained this to Gilly she laughed rather bitterly.

'I realise that now,' she said. 'The stories he used to tell me! He even said he was a hero in the Falklands War and had received a medal from the

72

Queen. It turns out he's never even been in the army.'

'Believe me,' I told her, 'baby or no baby you're better off without him. It's his wife you should feel sorry for.'

Gilly had her baby, a beautiful little girl, and now they are happily settled with a man Gilly met through a computer dating agency. These days she is only too glad she had nothing further to do with her lying fiancé.

The ideal partner

Having listed so many bad types I feel it only right to include an example of a person who was absolutely right for a committed relationship. Sean was a chef. He was a slim, friendly man and he came to see me originally about a financial matter which was worrying him. As it turned out Sean had got himself into a state where he couldn't see the wood for the trees and the financial problem wasn't all that difficult to solve.

Having got that out of the way Sean admitted there was something else on his mind. He was in love with a married woman, he confessed, and he wanted to know if the relationship would succeed. I looked carefully at his hand and I realised that here was a man who was made for a long, caring partnership.

Next to his heart line was a second fainter line running parallel to it. This was the classic double heart line found in warm-hearted home-lovers. Sean's fingers were small and plump, showing that he was a sensuous man with a love of good food and comfort, but they were also straight, emphasising his complete honesty. His heart line ended under the first finger of Jupiter indicating that he was loyal and considerate and his life line wound round his mount of Venus in a wide curve denoting a kind, loving nature and a craving for affection. There was no doubt that Sean would blossom given a cosy home and family

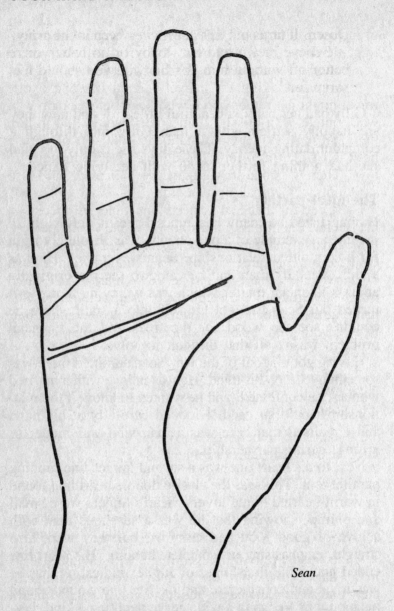

Sean

of his own. If he could find the right woman with whom to settle down he would be a wonderful provider and a generous and sympathetic husband and father.

A woman looking for a lively social life and exotic travel might get rather bored with Sean but a person who was content with blissful domesticity would find in him the ideal partner. Having established the sort of person he was I went on to look for signs of Sean's fortunes in love. There was one strong marriage indicated, but I also saw hints of a break-up to come.

I felt certain that Sean's need for someone special in his life had led him to pin his hopes on the wrong person. It looked as if his romance with the married woman would come to an end quite soon. Then, suddenly, in a flash of clairvoyance, I saw the girl he would marry. As I stared into his palm I saw the face of a very attractive girl. She had blue eyes which lit up when she smiled and dark hair flecked with gold. I described her to an incredulous Sean.

'She sounds gorgeous,' laughed Sean, 'but I've never met anyone like that.'

'Well, you will do and it won't be long now,' I assured him.

I don't think he believed a word of it. Yet three weeks later he rang me in amazement.

'You made it happen, I know you did,' he teased. 'I met her last Saturday. She's exactly as you described. We've only been out together four times but we feel as if we've known each other for years.'

Anne was a pretty blue-eyed nurse with blonde streaks in her dark brown hair. They fell in love almost immediately and were married six months later. The last I heard they were deliriously happy and planning a family. I'm quite sure they will have a long and successful marriage. Sean, of course, was a born homemaker with the homemaker's typical hand. Women can be born homemakers too and their hands would be very similar to Sean's, although probably smaller and more feminine in outline.

CHAPTER FIVE:
PHYSICAL LOVE: ARE YOU COMPATIBLE IN BED?

There is no doubt that sex is one of the most powerful, if not the most powerful, of all human urges. Counsellors often say that couples argue most frequently about money or children. Perhaps they do, but judging from the thousands of people I've seen over the years, the single factor which breaks up more marriages than anything else, is sex.

The strong attraction which binds couples together in the early days of their relationship seems to get swamped by the pressures and drudgery of day to day life and soon their sex life suffers. Perhaps those quarrels about money and children are simply a symptom of a deeper dissatisfaction. A dissatisfaction with their love life.

Again, the statistics tell us that it is wives, and not husbands, who most frequently decide on divorce and that wives are just as likely to have affairs as their husbands. Yet I know from the countless abandoned wives who come to my door that in the real world — or at least the world I live in — husbands are more likely to stray. Perhaps it is the wife who subsequently instigates the divorce, but only because she can't tolerate her husband's behaviour any longer. But wherever the fault lies, the break-up of a long standing relationship is always traumatic and where there are children involved it can even do lasting damage. There is so much unhappiness and guilt on both sides that you can't help wondering why we put ourselves through it.

Of course, sometimes couples find they have made a genuine mistake. They are unsuited and they really should never have got together in the first place. But I'm convinced that just as often, people (and men in particular) stray out of sheer boredom. The sad thing is that nine times out of ten they could find happiness in their own beds if only they'd put their heart and soul into it. Instead of using their imagination and working hard to improve things at home, they move to a new partner to save themselves the bother. Unfortunately unless they're careful, the very same problems might reoccur in a few years' time as the novelty of the relationship wears off. There are cases though, where no amount of imagination and discussion can possibly help. These are the cases where one partner is trying to go against his or her fundamental sexual nature.

Homosexual men and lesbian women often marry members of the opposite sex in the vain hope that somehow things will work out all right in the end. Bisexuals do the same in the belief that they can hide or suppress altogether the other side of their nature. And though the experts may not agree with me I'm quite convinced that there are some people, men as well as women, who are completely frigid and not suited to a sexual union of any kind. So, before trying to achieve the impossible with a partner it's worth studying their hand to see if they fall into any of these groups.

The homosexual hand

I've come across two basic types of homosexual hand and I saw an example of the first type late last year. Jane, an attractive young wife, came to see me about an embarrassing personal problem which she'd been unable to confide to anyone, not even her parents. Her heart line was blurred by dozens of stress lines so I knew that her problem was an emotional one.

At last Jane confessed that although she'd been married several weeks the marriage had never been consumated. Her husband, charming and considerate in every other way either made an excuse, changed the subject or, when cornered, simply refused to discuss it. He was a good man, Jane insisted and not selfish. He helped her around the house. He would cook a meal, vacuum the flat or iron a pile of shirts without complaint and he was an interesting companion. But Jane needed more. She couldn't decide whether there was something wrong with her, or something wrong with him. But whichever it was they were unlikely to find out because he wouldn't hear of consulting the doctor or marriage guidance counsellors.

'In a case like this I really need to see his hands,' I told Jane.

But Jane didn't think she could persuade him to come.

'The only alternative is a hand print then,' I went on.

Jane agreed to try to get one. Goodness knows how she did it but a few days later she appeared again with two photocopies.

When I looked at them it wasn't difficult to see what was wrong. Her husband was homosexual. His heart line burst out into two branches. One leapt up towards the fingers, the other turned back on itself so that it resembled a fishing hook. This is an absolutely unmistakable sign and shows that the subject desires to make love to members of his own sex. Naturally Jane was not eager to accept this explanation and since she was happy enough with her husband in other respects she didn't want to do anything hasty. She went home, said nothing and carried on as before. But it couldn't last. Six months later she

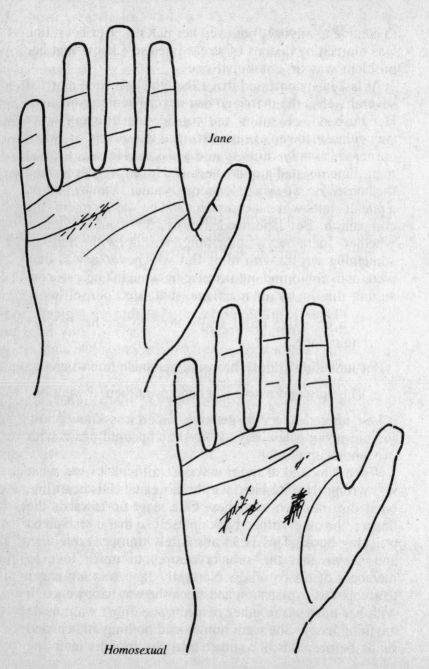

Jane

Homosexual

80

came home unexpectedly early from work and found her husband in bed with his male lover. The marriage was annulled.

Jane's husband had what I think of as the 'masculine' type of homosexual hand. These men are often kind and thoughtful and extremely talented. Their palms are frequently covered in a mass of tiny hair lines, showing that they are born worriers. The other type of homosexual hand I call the 'feminine hand'. These men have feminine tendencies and often like to dress as women. When you look at this type of palm the heart line ends in a branch like that of type one, one branch going up towards the fingers while the other turns back towards the head line. The head line is straight but the line is marred by islands showing a lack of concentration. Such men are frequently artistic and talented but sadly many of them lead lonely lives. They find it difficult to make lasting friendships and their lack of concentration often prevents them from putting their talents to good use.

The lesbian hand

This palm is very similar to the feminine type of homosexual hand and I saw it recently when two young women came for a consultation. At first I assumed they were friends or workmates but when I looked into their hands I realised that in fact they were lovers and well suited to each other. Like the feminine homosexual their heart lines ended in a distinct fork with one branch reaching to the fingers and the other going down on to the head line, showing a preference for their own sex in love. Unlike the homosexual, however, their head lines were clear and unmarred.

This pair were lucky enough to have smooth, unlined hands, showing that they had come to terms with their sexuality and suffered no anxiety because of it. They were

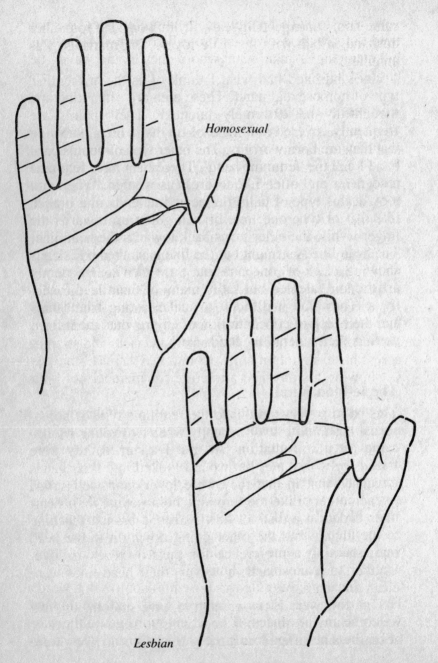

Homosexual

Lesbian

very wise to have recognised their preferences and not tried to force themselves into so-called 'normal' behaviour by marrying a man with whom they could never be entirely happy.

The bisexual man

The bisexual hand is more common than you might think and in these days of Aids, many heterosexual people consider it important to know if their partners have bisexual tendencies. This doesn't mean of course that a man with bisexual tendencies will necessarily make love to people of both sexes — but he will feel the attraction.

I saw such a case in the hand of a prominent businessman who came to see me, ostensibly about a partnership he was thinking of setting up. We dealt with his financial affairs first and I said nothing about the fact that I'd noticed his heart line began at the outer side of his palm in a series of tiny hair lines giving the appearance almost of a fan. The line then continued clear and straight across his hand until it burst out into two distinct branches — showing his physical attraction for members of both sexes.

It was clear however that there was stress ahead, connected with both business and relationships because the tell tale grilles dotted his success line (see my previous book *Your Hand in Business*) and his heart line. I felt sure that the two matters were closely related and that my client wouldn't get his business affairs running smoothly until he'd sorted out his love life. Eventually he admitted that he was strongly attracted to the man who was about to become his business partner but didn't know whether to make his feelings plain.

Psychically I was able to advise him not to say a word. His partner was strictly heterosexual and would not welcome any advances. If he let emotions get in the way of business he risked losing the partnership and everything

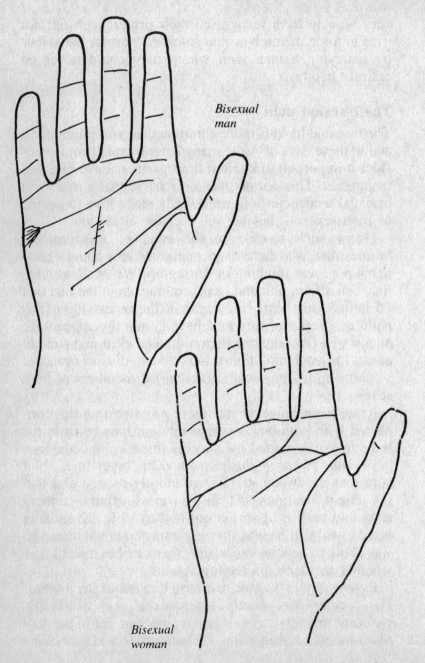

Bisexual man

Bisexual woman

he'd worked for for so long. The businessman took my advice and since then he's become a regular client. He keeps his private life and his business life totally separate and the partnership is flourishing.

The bisexual woman

Surprisingly enough the bisexual woman is usually married and unaware of her dual sexuality until something goes wrong with the relationship. It's amazing how many shell-shocked husbands I see who can't believe that their wife has left them for another woman — after years of apparently happy marriage.

The heart line of the bisexual woman is similar to that of the bisexual man, except that there is a conspicuous island at the beginning of the line where it joins the outside edge of the palm. The line then settles down and moves across the hand where it divides again into two branches, one ending tightly between the first and second fingers of Jupiter and Saturn, the other swooping down towards the head line.

As I explained earlier, since these women are also attracted to men, they often marry and if the marriage remains happy they might never discover that they are bisexual. I remember a young mother called Sally who came to see me because she was miserable about her husband's job. The couple had been together eight years, they had two lovely children and everything had been wonderful until her husband had been made redundant.

He was out of work for a time and then managed to get a night job. The money was very good, he quickly adjusted to the new sleep patterns and as far as he was concerned it was the ideal solution. Sally, unfortunately, thought differently. Although at first she was just grateful for some regular money coming in she soon tired of the situation. She hated sitting alone night after night and then creeping about during the day while her husband slept.

'I can't even use the vacuum cleaner because it's too noisy,' she complained, 'and I can't do the housework at night because then I wake the children.'

However it was the loneliness that upset her far more than the housework and, of course, the couple's sex life almost dwindled away because they were never available at the same time. I could see that there were problems ahead and also that Sally had a typical bisexual heart line. Yet there was no rival on the scene at the moment and I felt there might be a chance that the couple could patch things up if they acted quickly. I suggested that if Sally's husband really couldn't change his job, then they should at least set aside some time exclusively for each other every week.

'Get a friend to collect the children from school one afternoon a week,' I said, 'so that you and your husband can go out together or stay in together. . . You could do the same for her on a different afternoon.'

Sally said she'd try. Sadly, she didn't try hard enough. Perhaps she didn't realise the seriousness of the problem, or perhaps subconsciously she had tired of the marriage. Whatever the reason, things continued to slide in the household. Then out of the blue, an old woman friend of Sally's who had lived in America for years suddenly turned up on the doorstep one evening.

Naturally Sally was delighted to see her and she was also glad of the company. The woman knew few people in the area, Sally was lonely, and gradually they took to spending almost every evening together. Sally's husband didn't mind at all. In fact he was pleased. It was better to see Sally cheerful than wandering around with a long face after hours on her own. One of the things Sally missed was the occasional night out. It was very difficult to get baby-sitters and she couldn't really afford it. Instead her friend sometimes brought round a bottle of wine and a take-away meal and they had a merry evening. Then one night the friend had rather more than usual to drink and couldn't drive home.

> 'Never mind,' said Sally. 'You can stay here.'
> 'Well don't bother about making up a bed specially for me,' said her friend, 'I'll share yours.'

Sally, of course, had a large double bed, one half of which was empty, and the suggestion was probably innocent enough. Yet her friend clearly had bisexual tendencies too. When they shared the bed one thing led to another and they became lovers. The first I heard of it was when Sally's husband came to see me a year later. His wife had run off with a woman friend, he told me, leaving him to bring up the children. She never came back.

The sadist

Often I'm invited to hotels or private functions to read the palms of the guests present. It's usually very light hearted and each person who wants one receives a short five minute mini-reading. I always remember that other people are probably listening so I'm careful not to say anything embarrassing.

Sometimes of course I come across complicated problems that can't be dealt with in a few minutes, in which case I suggest that if they're interested, the subject should come to me later for a full length consultation. At other times I come across hands that make me feel five minutes is much too long and I'm dying to get away from them as soon as possible. I came across this sort of hand at an office party one Christmas. The assistant manager suddenly put his glass down and thrust his palm under my nose.

> 'All right then, what do you make of that!' he said, chuckling.

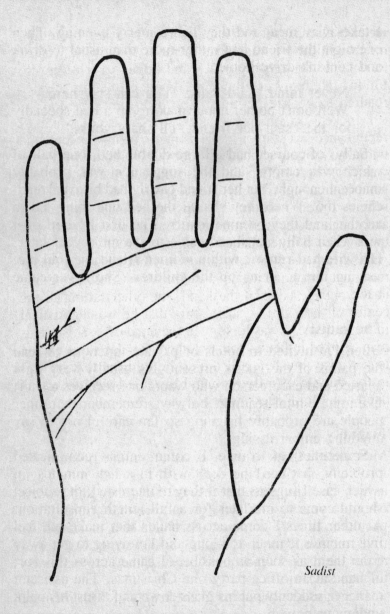

Sadist

He had already set my hackles rising earlier by telling me that palmistry was a load of rubbish. Now he wanted to put me through my paces and hoped to trip me up. I didn't like him but I thought I'd better give him a quick reading to get rid of him.

I picked up his hand and as I did so a wave of repugnance swept over me. The man's palm was long and wide, his fingers short and stubby. His mount of Venus was flat, the life line falling straight to the base of the hand with no curve at all. He clearly was cold and selfish with no time for others. The tips of his fingers were hard and ended in strange little points (not to be confused with the overall pointed hand), a sign of cruelty.

His head line was long, showing that he was a clever man, but it divided into two distinct branches, one going to the outside edge of the hand, the other falling to the centre of the palm — suggesting that he was egotistical in the extreme. I was looking at the hand of a sadist. This man enjoyed inflicting pain on others. I made some excuse to get away but before I did so he told me that he was in the middle of a divorce and that his love life wasn't happy. I could guess why.

Frigidity

Most people think of frigidity as a feminine problem but I'm firmly convinced that men are just as likely to be frigid as women. I have seen plenty of frigid men and women over the years and I'm not even sure that frigidity is a problem. It only becomes a problem if a frigid person finds themself involved with a lusty partner, or if they are made to feel inadequate because they are genuinely uninterested in sex.

The signs are the same in the hands of both men and women, although obviously male hands are usually heavier than female hands. Frigid hands tend to be quite smooth with very few fine lines. The head and heart lines

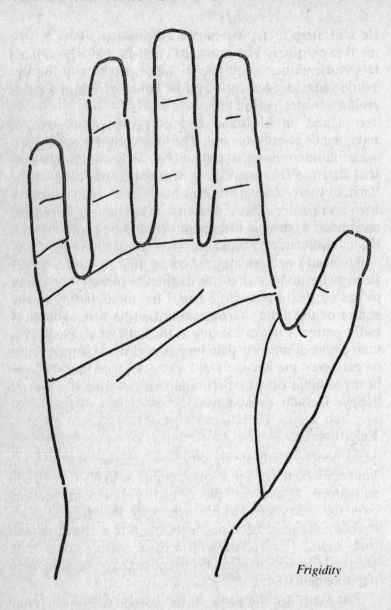

Frigidity

are close together, showing narrow mindedness where sex is concerned. The heart line runs in a shallow curve across the palm, the mount of Venus is flat and the life line straight suggesting physical coldness and the palm itself feels very stiff to the touch. There is no elasticity in it. These hands are thin and almost wasted in appearance, the fingers fleshless and rather scrawny. Quite often the head line is long, showing that these people channel all their energies into mental rather than physical pursuits.

There can be many reasons for frigidity. It would take a psychiatrist to explain it all, I suppose, but I saw a case recently where the cause seemed obvious even to a layman. A brother and sister came to see me. They were middle aged and had lived with a domineering mother all their lives. Now their mother had died and there were problems with her will. Could I see the outcome of the legal battles going on, they wanted to know. This was fairly simple to sort out but in the course of examining their hands I noticed that they were both typical frigid types. Their mother had been obsessed with hygiene and brought them up to believe that sex was dirty.

Now in their middle years, neither one of them had ever had a sexual relationship or appeared to want one. They both still lived at home and planned to continue to do so. I could see that their future happiness lay with each other, yet there was nothing improper in their relationship. Affection was enough for both of them and in their own way they were happy. Curiously enough, the sign of physical coldness − straight life line and flat mount of Venus − is also a sign of general meanness, and in the course of the conversation the cause of their main disagreements came out.

'He will use my butter,' complained the sister. 'And if he runs out of something he takes the things I buy. That's the only time we ever argue.'

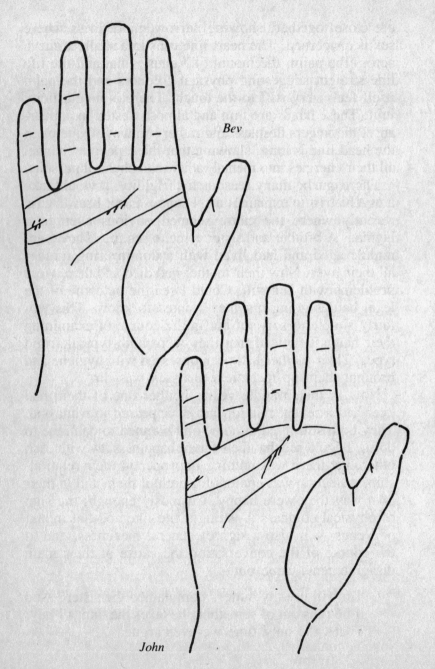

Bev

John

PHYSICAL LOVE: ARE YOU COMPATIBLE IN BED?

It turned out that they bought their own separate food, had their own separate cooking utensils and prepared their meals separately. The idea of sharing had clearly never crossed their minds. They both guarded their own possessions jealously and became very annoyed at any borrowing.

Every couple argues about something though, and despite these minor squabbles the brother and sister lived amicably under the same roof. The brother's hand was just as frigid as his sister's and there was no marriage indicated. They returned to the home they shared with every intention of continuing their way of life. I expect they are still there to this day, each guarding his own butter but happy enough in their own way.

Getting out of a rut

Having made sure a potential partner has the same sexual outlook as you doesn't mean that you need never think about your sex life again. Of course love comes naturally, but unfortunately the pressures and strains of life sometimes get in the way. Long term partners fall into a routine and no longer put the imagination and effort into their love lives that once they did. If the situation continues the relationship can deteriorate and this is when one or both partners might be tempted to stray.

The trouble is, it's all too easy to get into a rut without even knowing you're there. How can you tell if your loved one is dissatisfied? Particularly when this is just the sort of thing he or she is unlikely to talk about. The answer of course is to look at their hand.

I saw the tell tale signs quite clearly in the palms of a nice young married couple who visited me the other evening. Beverley and John were very happy together. They were childhood sweethearts who'd sat next to each other at school and had been inseparable ever since. Nobody could imagine these two ever parting. They were

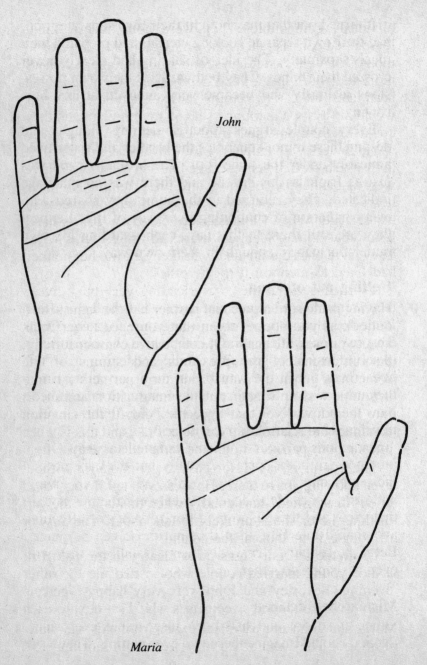

John

Maria

obviously compatible. They were both honest, kind, loving and considerate as shown by their well developed mounts of Venus, soft hands and straight fingers. What's more they both had a good gap between their heart and head lines, indicating a strong sense of humour. This pair would always see the funny side of any problem and they could laugh about their troubles.

Yet Beverley's hand was marred by a series of tiny fret lines which blurred her marriage line and heart line. There were also a number of downward lines running from her heart line. This showed very clearly disappointments in her sex life. When I looked more closely at John's hand I saw that he had identical marks to those of his wife. They were both dissatisfied with their sex life but neither had liked to mention it to the other.

It turned out that they were leading very busy lives, they were often tired and one area was bound to suffer. It seemed almost impossible to find time for love. Once they realised that this was a problem it wasn't difficult to solve. Instead of spending evenings catching up on the housework they'd been unable to do at any other time, they cut down on the chores and spent more time in bed. Now the house doesn't always look its best but their relationship is in first class condition.

Sometimes, of course, it's not as simple as that. Often a couple are both 'normal' sexually but they are nevertheless incompatible. Some people need a lot of loving and some don't. If the difference between them is not all that great and there is a good bond, plenty of affection and shared interests, then a compromise can be made. But if the couple differ wildly then it is unlikely they will ever be happy together.

Mismatched desires

Maria and John are a typical example of this sad state of affairs. They met when they were both working for

95

the same company. Maria was a pretty young Italian girl and John fell for her the moment he saw her. Their relationship developed slowly. They got to know each other in the office, shared every lunch hour and they were very good friends before they eventually became lovers.

Maria's parents were strict and the couple had few chances to make love, but there was nothing to suggest that there was anything wrong. Three years after their first meeting John and Maria got married. They were very happy when they moved into their own small home. They were in love and seemed well suited in every way.

What neither of them realised was that Maria was a maternal, rather than a sensuous, woman and every time they went to bed together she was subconsciously hoping to conceive. At first, of course, it was out of the question. Two wage packets were needed to pay the mortgage but eighteen months later they both agreed that they could now afford to start a family. Maria became pregnant almost at once and she was thrilled. When their baby daughter was born nine months later Maria's joy was complete. Now she had everything she wanted.

Unfortunately John did not. Suddenly his wife didn't want to make love any more. At first he thought she was tired with the demands of a tiny baby. But as the months moved into a year, then two years, and the situation didn't improve he realised that there was something seriously wrong. They came to see me and looking at their hands it was obvious that nice as they were, they weren't suited sexually. John was an ardent, warm hearted lover. He had the traces of a girdle of Venus, his mount of Venus was fleshy and full and his heart line ended on the mount of Jupiter. Maria on the other hand had very thin fingers, a thin, pale heart line, a mount of Venus that was almost flat and no girdle of Venus at all. She simply wasn't interested in sex. She thought of it simply as a necessary chore to be gone through in order to conceive children.

I'm sorry to say that there was little I could do to help them. They persevered with the marriage for another year but eventually the inevitable happened. John met someone else who could satisfy him in bed and he parted from Maria. Strangely enough Maria was relieved. Now she no longer had to invent excuses. She could live at peace with her child and see John from time to time when he came to visit his daughter. They divorced. John married his new love, but Maria remains single to this day. I think she always will.

Mirror images

In general the more similar a couple's hands the more compatible they are likely to be. The size of the hand is immaterial, it is the shape and the pattern of lines on the palm which count. Now, of course, no two hands are exactly alike, so there's no need to panic if your hand is not identical to your partner's. The important point is that the lines and shapes on the palm are similar.

A man with a wide mount of Venus should not marry a woman with a narrow mount and a woman with a short heart line should not marry a man with a long heart line. One half of the pair would crave physical affection while the other would long to be left alone. They could never be happy together. Fortunately, the possible combinations of compatible partners is endless but to illustrate what I mean I've included a few examples I've seen amongst my clients.

Mr A & Miss B

Mr A's heart line reaches up towards the fingers of Jupiter and Saturn showing a jealous streak. He is likely to be rather possessive with anyone he cares for. He has a strong sexual drive which is evident from his broken girdle of Venus and his mount of Venus. The life line

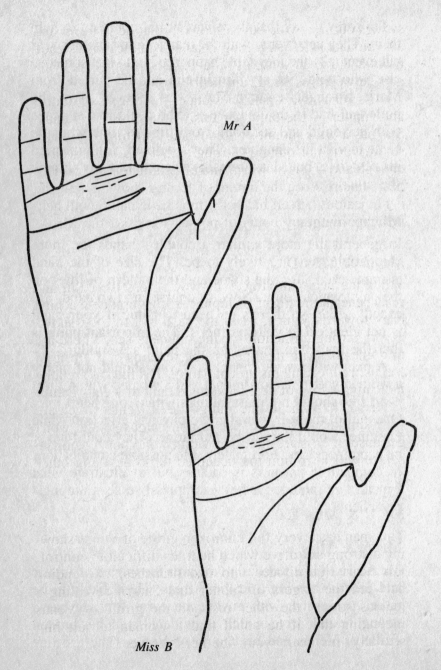

Mr A

Miss B

swings out in a wide curve showing that he is warm and affectionate. He has a long head line indicating a good brain and a keen sense of humour as shown by the wide gap between his head and heart lines.

Miss B has two small lines under the fingers of Saturn and Jupiter — the only remains of the girdle of Venus. She has a wide mount of Venus and soft fingertips. Her sex drive is not quite as strong as Mr A's but it's close enough and she is as warm and affectionate as he is. Her heart line rests on the mount of Jupiter showing that she is not jealous herself but her sympathetic nature will help her cope with any bouts of possessiveness from Mr A.

Mr C & Miss D

When the heart line traces its way across the palm and rests beneath the finger of Jupiter, with a branch reaching back towards Saturn, as in the case of Mr C, it shows a very strong attraction for the opposite sex. There are fine lines beneath the fingers, the remains of a girdle of Venus, reinforcing his ardent nature. His fingers are long indicating a love of detail and his mount of Venus is full.

Miss D has a head line and girdle of Venus which are very similar to Mr C's. She is not jealous so she won't get upset if he stares at other women and her passionate nature will keep him too occupied to do anything other than look.

Mr E & Miss F

This man has a very full unbroken girdle of Venus showing a strong sex drive which he finds difficult to control. His heart line divides into two branches, one ending between the fingers of Jupiter and Saturn revealing a jealous streak, the other rests on the girdle of Venus indicating that if he could find a woman to suit him sexually, his heart would be hers forever.

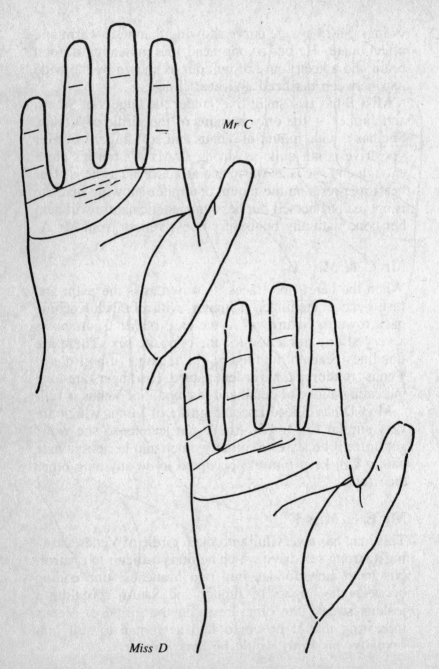

Mr C

Miss D

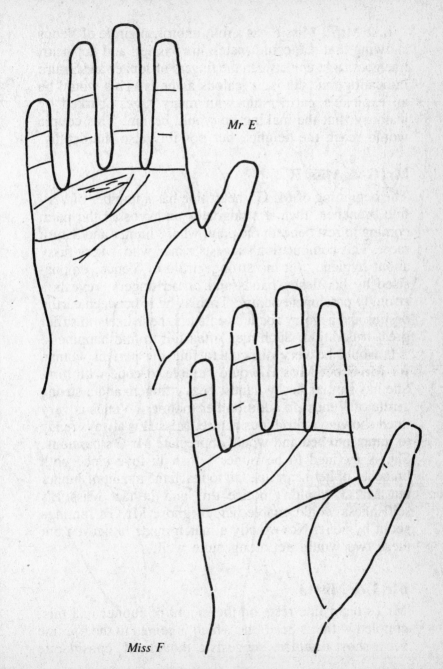

Mr E

Miss F

Like Mr E, Miss F has a full, unbroken girdle of Venus showing that she could match his passion and her heart line goes right up between the fingers of Jupiter and Saturn indicating that she is as jealous as he is. This would be an explosive partnership with many rages sparked by jealousy, but the making up would be fun. This couple would reach the heights, but possibly also the depths.

Mr G & Miss H

The beginning of Mr G's heart line has a number of very fine branches, then it straightens and crosses the palm coming to rest beneath the point where Jupiter and Saturn meet. This combination suggests a man who is very fussy about hygiene, yet his strong girdle of Venus, emphasised by his fleshy hands and broad fingers, reveals a strongly passionate nature. Torn as he is between earthy desires and a worry about cleanliness, he is likely to suffer great frustration. Such men often fail to find happiness.

It would be very difficult to find the perfect woman for Mr G but Miss H would be able to cope with him. She has similar fleshy hands, heavy fingers and a strong girdle of Venus. In addition her mount of Venus is very lined showing a flirtatious nature. Miss H is always ready to jump into bed and would appreciate Mr G's passions. She is inclined to be rather selfish in love since both branches of her heart line fail to reach the mount of Jupiter but Mr G wouldn't notice this and in fact Miss H's selfishness would enable her to ignore Mr G's rantings about hygiene. Not exactly a match made in heaven but these two would get along quite well.

Mr I & Miss J

Mr I's heart line rests on the mount of Jupiter and this, coupled with his head line which is joined to the life line for a short distance, suggests a thoughtful, considerate

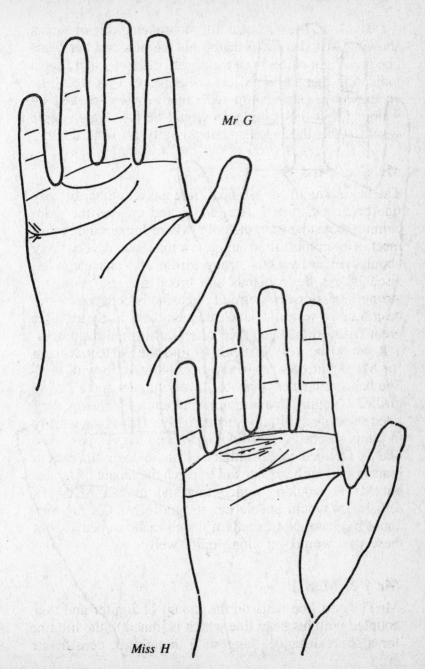

Mr G

Miss H

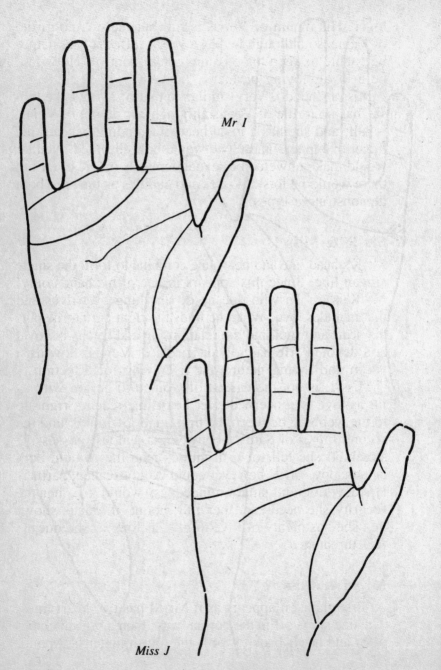

Mr I

Miss J

104

lover. His mount of Venus is full but there is no girdle of Venus so although he has a warm, affectionate nature he is able to keep his passions under control. He would be a loyal, loving partner.

Miss J's hand is very similar to that of Mr I. Like him she has no girdle of Venus although her mount of Venus is full, and she has a loyal heart line ending beneath the finger of Jupiter. These two would be well suited. Neither would make unwelcome sexual demands on the other but there would be lots of kisses and cuddles as they are both demonstrative types.

Mr K & Miss L

Mr K's head line and heart line combine to form the single simian line. Since this appears in one of his hands only, Mr K is a man who doesn't do anything by halves and that includes love. When he finds the right partner he puts his heart and soul into the relationship and he can be loyal and devoted. He has a wide girdle of Venus showing a warm and loving nature and a craving for affection.

Miss L is not the easiest of women to get on with as far as love is concerned. Her heart line reaches right up to the webbing between the first finger of Jupiter and the second finger of Saturn, betraying a jealous, possessive streak. If she fell for a flirtatious man they would both be unhappy. Mr K however could be an excellent partner. His devotion and single mindedness would give her the security she needs and her full mount of Venus shows that she has plenty of love to give as long as she doesn't feel threatened.

Mr M & Miss N

At first glance it appears as if Mr M has two heart lines. The line starts off in the normal way, then a branch comes off it and heads back towards the fourth finger of Apollo.

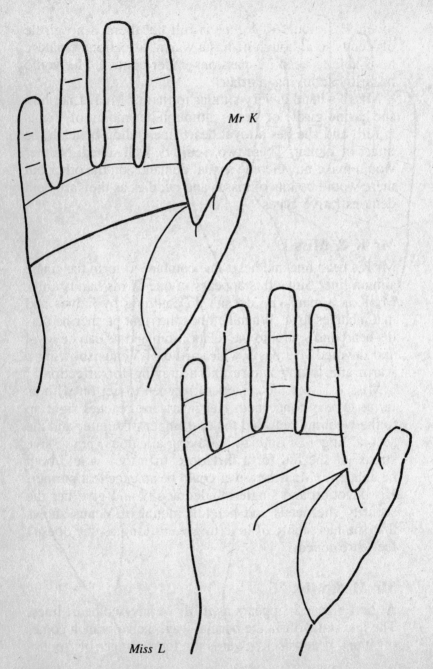

Mr K

Miss L

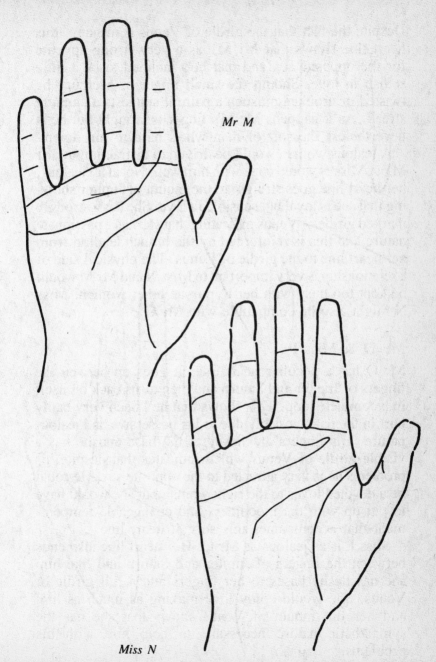

Mr M

Miss N

Despite the fact that the girdle of Venus is missing, this heart line shows that Mr M has a very strong appetite for the opposite sex and that he's inclined to be a little selfish in love. Should the small finger of Mercury be twisted or crooked on such a palm it suggests a cunning streak. As it happens Mr M's finger is straight but he is nevertheless the sort of man who's hard to pin down.

A jealous woman would be driven to distraction by Mr M but Miss N would cope with him well. Not at all jealous, her heart line goes straight to the mount of Jupiter showing that she is loyal but sensible in love. She has a strongly marked girdle of Venus indicating that she has a passionate nature and this is reinforced by the branch leading from her heart line to the girdle of Venus. The physical side of a relationship is very important to Miss N and Mr M would be kept too busy with her to pursue other women. Miss N might also be compatible with Mr G.

Mr O & Miss P

Mr O has a peculiar heart line. It goes up between the fingers of Jupiter and Saturn and then turns back on itself in a complete loop. This shows that he's been very badly hurt in the past, possibly due to his possessive and jealous nature. His fingers are fleshy at the base and he has a visible girdle of Venus which indicates that despite his problems he is very attracted to the opposite sex. He could be a devoted lover to the right woman but she would have to put up with the moodiness and changeable temperament that accompanies this sort of heart line.

Miss P is as jealous as Mr O. Her heart line also ends between the fingers of Jupiter and Saturn and like him she has fleshy bases to her fingers and a full girdle of Venus. She would enjoy love making as much as him and her full mount of Venus shows that she has the sympathetic nature necessary to help him with his problems.

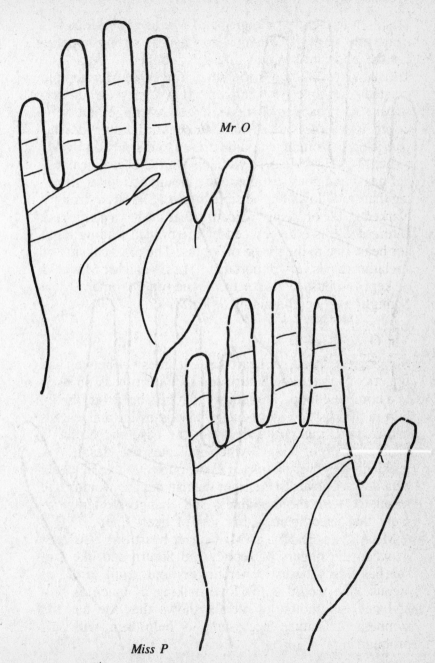

Mr O

Miss P

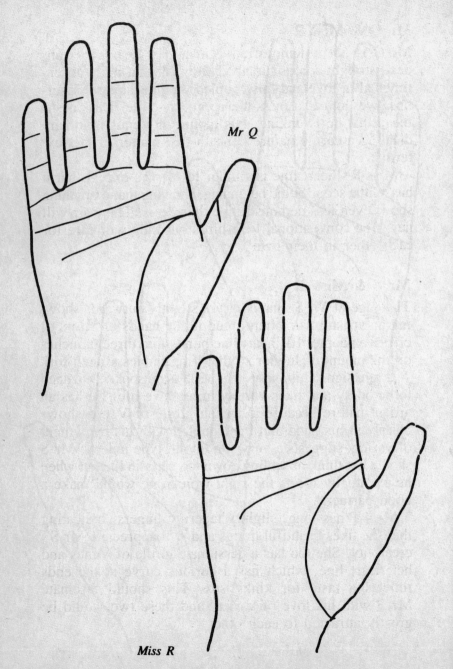

Mr Q

Miss R

Mr Q & Miss R

Mr Q is not a demonstrative man. His heart line runs dead straight across his hand showing that he is unsentimental in love and this coupled with his square fingertips gives him a business-like approach to life. This doesn't mean that he is unkind. His mount of Venus is full indicating a caring nature beneath that matter of fact exterior.

Miss R's heart line is similar to Mr Q's except that it has a little scoop at the beginning, showing that if anything she is even less demonstrative than he is. This pair will never be conventional love birds but they will care for each other in their own way.

Mr S & Miss T

The edge of Mr S's hand curves slightly outwards showing an artistic flair often found in the hands of actors or creative people. His heart line bursts into three branches on the mount of Jupiter so that it resembles a pitch fork − a rare sign. This shows that Mr S is outspoken, inclined to be bossy and likes variety in his love life. He has an ardent nature because a broken girdle of Venus shows clearly in his hand and this coupled with his enjoyment of variety suggests a very fun loving type indeed. Mr S should not think of settling down too early in life but when he eventually meets the right woman he would make a good partner.

Miss T has long, slightly tapering fingers, indicating that she likes beautiful things and will appreciate Mr S's creativity. She too has a passionate girdle of Venus and her heart line, which has a curious curve at the ends reflects a taste for kinky sex. This should fascinate Mr S with his love of variety and these two would be greatly attracted to each other.

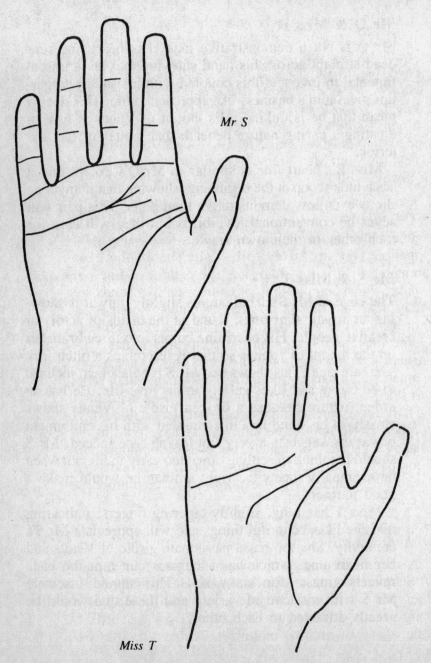

Mr S

Miss T

CHAPTER SIX:
THE MARRIAGE M

Being a palmist is rather like being a doctor — as soon as people find out what you do they want to be diagnosed. Wherever I go I tend to get hands thrust under my nose. A few years ago I had to go into hospital for an operation and I spent more time reading palms (for the doctors and nurses as well as the patients), than I did being treated. Yet the funny thing is I never get bored with it. Once you start looking at them, hands become endlessly fascinating and sooner or later all my friends and aquaintances succumb to my curiosity.

It was in this way and quite by chance that I discovered that my old friend Helen was the lucky possessor of what I call the perfect Marriage 'M'. Helen had just moved house and she decided to get rid of all the junk she'd accumulated over the years by taking it along to a car boot sale. Her husband Don was working that day so knowing that I have a weakness for markets, sales and anything of that kind, she asked if I'd like to go along to help.

Naturally I was delighted. We took blankets and flasks of tea because it was a cold day and we set up our stall early in the morning. Maybe it was the weather or maybe it was lack of advertising but the sale got off to a slow start. Helen and I sat there drinking tea, not a customer

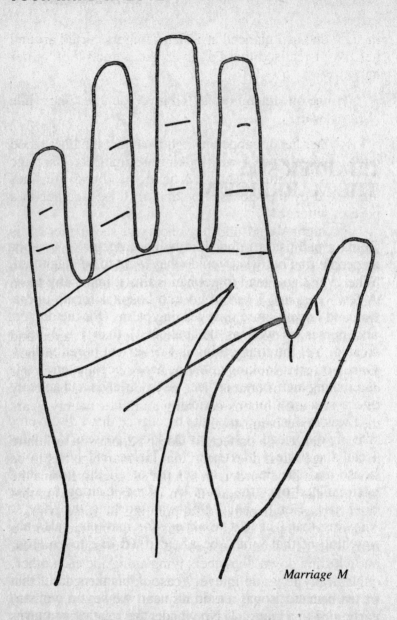

Marriage M

in sight and as I glanced at Helen's fingers curled around her mug I realised that I'd never had a good look at her hand.

> 'Come on Helen,' I said, 'I'll give you a reading while we wait.'

I took her hand, cupped it slightly so that the lines stood out and all at once I was looking at a perfect marriage 'M'. This is formed when the heart, head and life lines are linked by the success line and all flow together in a perfect letter 'M'.

This might sound odd but once you see it the 'M' is unmistakable. Unfortunately a perfect M is a rare sign, often the success line joins the heart line too far down its length to produce a properly formed letter, but when the shape is perfect the bearer is assured of a wonderfully happy marriage.

I knew that Helen and Don were very well suited and this confirmed it. They met when they were both in their teens and had been inseparable ever since. They have their disagreements of course, like any couple, but basically they enjoy each other's company and after twenty years they still love being together.

The absence of a perfect 'M' doesn't doom you to failure in marriage but it does mean that the marriage has to be worked at a little harder. When the success line joins the heart line a little distance down its length it means that the marriage will prove disappointing in some way.

Oddly enough I have seen this sign combined with a heart line which ends just above it in several branches, one pointing down, the others lying alongside each other, quite a lot lately and in every case it has turned out that the woman (for some reason it's nearly always a woman) is married to a bisexual. No wonder the relationship turns out to be a disappointment.

Sadly a great many people seem to marry for the wrong

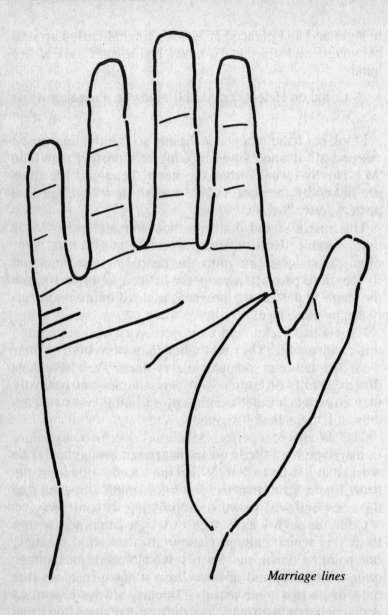

Marriage lines

reasons. Even today it's amazing how many clients I see who married primarily because they were afraid of being left on the shelf — men as well as women, so perhaps it's not surprising that such a high percentage of marriages end in divorce. All this can be see on the hand.

Will you marry?

Marriage lines are found on the outer side of the palm beneath the little finger of Mercury. They are short, horizontal lines which begin on the edge of the palm and move inwards. Often to see them properly you need to crook your little finger slightly. Faint lines tend to indicate less important relationships, the deeper lines marriages. The more deep lines present, the more marriages are likely. I would expect someone like the much married Zsa Zsa Gabor, who has had eight husbands so far, to have a maze of short lines crammed on the mount of Mercury.

Incidentally these lines don't necessarily mean a wedding ring. Some people don't believe in the legal institution of marriage but live together as man and wife. To all intents and purposes couples like this are married and their relationship would show on the hand as a marriage line.

The lower on the hand the marriage line appears, the earlier in life the wedding. It's quite common to see two lines on a subject's hand, one very low and the other high up close to the base of the small finger. This is often seen on the hand of a person who has married too young, regretted it and steered clear of further legal entanglements until much later in life when they relent and try marriage once more. When the marriage line is strong and clear, reaching deep into the hand, it fortells an extremely happy marriage. This type of marriage line usually accompanies a perfect marriage 'M' .

I saw an example of this in the hands of Leslie and

his wife Beverley, a couple who have now become friends as well as clients. They both are blessed wth long, strong marriage lines and in fact they have been happily married for 17 years. They met quite by chance when they both went independently to Bournemouth for the weekend with friends. As luck would have it Leslie's friend had once dated Beverley and when they bumped into each other at the seaside the four young people joined forces. They had a merry time and at the end of the weekend Leslie took Beverley's telephone number.

They now believe that they were fated to fall in love. The following week Leslie phoned Beverley to ask her out but he could get no reply from the number at all. It was puzzling and disappointing. Perhaps she had given him the wrong number. Still, there was no great harm done. Leslie was not deeply involved and he was a sociable young man with a busy life. He shrugged his shoulders and prepared to forget the whole thing. But fate stepped in once again.

No young person stays in on Saturday night if they can help it and the next day being Saturday, Leslie went to a party. Who should he see as he walked in the door but Beverley. It turned out that her parents were away on holiday and rather than remain in the empty house on her own, she had gone to stay with her married sister — which is why there was no one to answer the phone.

The small misunderstanding sorted out they began dating and soon found that their minds were so in tune they often said the same thing at the same time. They were married eleven months after that first meeting and have been happy ever since.

If the marriage line turns up towards the small finger it suggests a loving partnership where marriage is barred for some reason. It might be that one half of the couple is not free to marry or that religion or the law might forbid it, as in the case of lesbians and homosexuals.

Reconciliation or separation?

Sometimes the marriage line is broken up. This suggests a breakdown in the marriage but if an overlapping line joins the two pieces, then a reconciliation is possible. After a successful reconciliation the break in the marriage line would disappear.

I saw this sign in the hands of Steve and Barbara, a couple who despite four healthy children and a ten year marriage finally decided they could no longer stay together. They parted and Barbara, miserable and unhappy, came to see me in the hope that I might predict better times ahead. When I looked at her hand I saw that although there was a break in her marriage line, a sister line ran alongside it, bridging the gap.

'I think you and your husband will get back together again,' I told her.

She shook her head bitterly. 'Oh no, no chance of that,' she insisted, 'I've had enough of him. Towards the end we couldn't even be in the same room without arguing.'

Barbara's heart line also showed a break and there was a clear cross on the line, indicating that the couple's problems had been financial. This was quite right. Apparently Steve ran his own small business and for the past year he'd been experiencing crippling cash flow problems. The stress had affected him badly and his moods, coupled with the financial strain, had been too much for the marriage. The couple had reached the point where they believed their feelings for each other had died and they parted.

'Well perhaps,' I told Barbara, 'but I still see you getting back together.'

She was highly sceptical. Yet eighteen months later, she returned to see me with her husband in tow. There

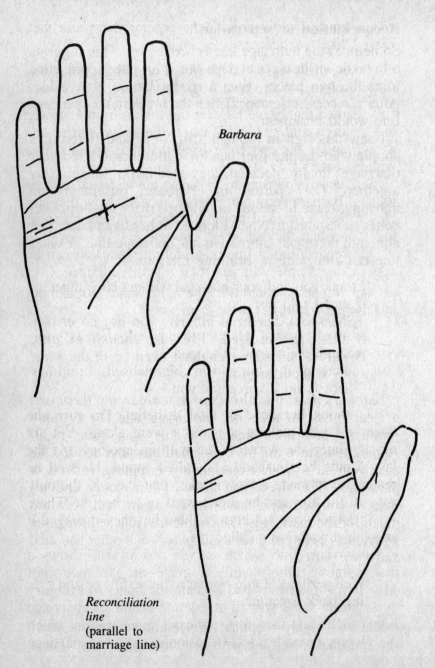

Barbara

*Reconciliation
line
(parallel to
marriage line)*

was a kind of glow around the pair of them and they looked like two teenagers in love.

'Yes, that's right,' said Barbara beaming. 'You knew all along. We're back together.'

It seemed that Steve had kept in touch in order to see his children and gradually when the initial anger had melted away, the couple realised that they couldn't live without each other.

Steve ended up losing his business but he found another job and Barbara went out to work as well. Now they are closer than ever and hoping to open a new business together when they've saved enough.

This reconciliation line is so definite that you can be certain the couple will get back together again.

One woman who had this line in her hand laughed out loud when I told her what it meant.

'Bettina, I must tell you that my divorce is going through right now,' she said.

'Perhaps it is but it won't be finalised,' I told her. 'There is no divorce for you.'

She shook her head in total disbelief. I'm sure she thought I was making it up as I went along. Yet six months later she wrote to me with an apology. At the last minute her husband had called round. He said he realised he'd made a big mistake, that she was the only woman for him and he didn't want to let her go. There was a lot to work out betwen them but they managed it and the divorce was called off.

A marriage line which curves downwards shows a disappointing union while a grille on the mount of Mercury — the fleshy pad beneath the finger of Mercury — suggests some sort of stress and strain. A marriage line which ends in a fork indicates a separation which is welcome on both sides. Occasionally a strong marriage

line is accompanied by a star on the mount of Jupiter.
This is the sign of a person who will marry into money.

In sickness and in health

People rarely think of consulting a palmist until they have
problems and those problems are often emotional. Even
bowler-hatted businessmen who arrive ostensibly to
discuss their company often end up confessing to marital
difficulties. In the course of my work I hear of so many
troubled marriages that it's easy to become cynical about
the whole institution. Yet whenever I become too
jaundiced, I think of my young neighbours, Breda and
Paul, who are a living example of courage and true love
despite enormous problems.

When they married four years ago life looked wonderful
for Breda and Paul. Paul had a good job, they moved
into a comfortable flat and within six months Breda was
pregnant. They both wanted children while they were
young and they were overjoyed when a perfect little
daughter was born. Everything should have been ideal.
Yet not long afterwards Paul began to suffer worrying
symptoms. It took some time for the doctors to discover
what was wrong with him and when they did, it was bad
news. Paul had multiple sclerosis, the disease which
attacks the nerves controlling the muscles of the body.

Today, the couple have two beautiful little daughters
but Paul can no longer work and he is confined to a
wheelchair. He finds the smallest tasks difficult and Breda
has to care for him constantly. Life isn't easy for either
of them, yet somehow their home is always full of
laughter and they are still obviously in love. Some women
couldn't cope with a husband as sick as Paul, but unwittingly when he married Breda, he chose a woman whose
loyalty and devotion would never falter no matter what
obstacles were thrown in her path.

Breda's palm contains a perfect marriage 'M'. Her

fingers are soft and her mount of Venus wide, showing a kind, sympathetic nature. Her heart line ends on the mount of Jupiter revealing her loyal temperament and her marriage line is strong and deep. Despite the problems they face, Breda will never let her husband down.

For his part, Paul is doing everything he can to help her. He puts on a cheerful face, he listens whenever Breda needs a grumble and he is determined to remain positive.

> 'I tell you what, Breda,' he says, 'I've made up my mind. By the time I'm thirty I'll be walking again. I'm certain I will.'

He is just 27 years old.

Love at first sight

Many people scoff at the idea of love at first sight, but I'm a firm believer in that romantic idea of eyes meeting across a crowded room and igniting instant chemistry. Surprisingly enough such encounters aren't all that rare and often end in marriage. When this is likely the marriage line runs almost in a semi circle round the base of the little finger of Mercury.

We often think of such encounters occuring only in the very young, yet I've found this sign more often in the hands of older people who've nearly given up all hope of marriage. In fact, I've even seen this line high up in the hands of widows approaching the age of sixty, so it just shows there's no need to give up whatever your age. The right person could be out there somewhere.

Is your lover faithful?

Tina was a rather silly girl. A typist of 23, she looked and acted years younger. Nevertheless she sported an enormous diamond ring on her engagement finger, of which she was obviously very proud and it was clear that she had marriage on her mind.

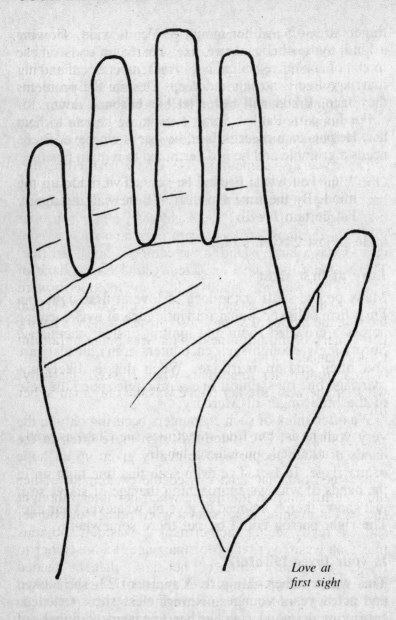

Love at
first sight

'Yes, my fiancé is ever so good,' she said. 'He saved for ages to buy this ring. Isn't it lovely? I chose it myself.' She paused and twisted the ring awkwardly. 'But the trouble is . . . that's all he seems to think about — saving. He's on about saving for a house now . . . when I think we should go out and enjoy ourselves while we're young.'

There was also something else Tina wasn't telling me. Or her fiancé for that matter. Her hands were broad, the bases of her fingers were fleshy and she had a strongly marked girdle of Venus. She was clearly a very sensuous girl. But the most striking feature as far as I was concerned was a large island in the centre of her heart line. This was not the sign I expected to find on the hand of a young girl who was madly in love and looking forward to her wedding. An island, together with a lot of vertical lines on the mount of Venus (also present in Tina's hand), is the mark of unfaithfulness. Tina was being unfaithful to her fiancé.

Tina studied her fingernails when I asked, tactfully, whether she was sure her fiancé was the only man in her life.

'Well he is, but I do sometimes see Chris as well,' she admitted, 'just for a laugh.'

It turned out that Tina missed the excitement of her old free life and on the nights when her fiancé thought she was at evening classes on a word processor course, she was really seeing another man. It was quite obvious that Tina wasn't yet ready for marriage. I advised her to forget saving for a while, tell her fiancé that she needed more time to think things over and not tie herself down till she was older. If anything, Tina was relieved. Immature as she was, in her heart of hearts she realised that if she married now, she'd probably end up divorced within a few years.

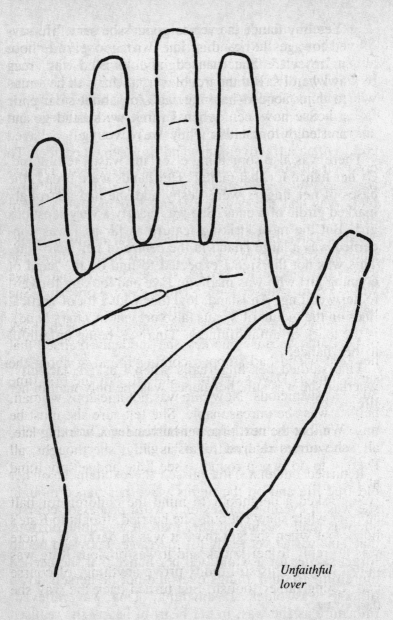

Unfaithful lover

Strangely enough the tell tale signs of unfaithfulness often show in the hand of the wronged partner too, although they are fainter and slightly blurred. I was struck by this when I saw the palm of a troubled young woman who had just ended her marriage in a rather dramatic fashion. Sue had been deeply in love with her husband and trusted him totally. They had two well behaved children, an attractive house and life seemed perfect. To crown it all Sue's husband Dave was promoted. The extra money was very welcome of course. The only problem was that the new job seemed to involve a lot of overtime.

First, Dave had to work late several nights a week. Then he started going in at weekends too. At about the same time the couple's sex life seemed to fizzle out. Dave was tired of course, with all that extra work, and Sue naturally made excuses for him.

Yet something must have been warning her at the back of her mind because one day she suddenly realised that her best friend had stopped coming round at about the same time as Dave's overtime started. For the first time Sue was suspicious. Now Sue was not a jealous woman, neither was she unreasonable. She felt sure she must be mistaken, but the next time her husband was working late, all her worries returned. This is silly, she thought, all I've got to do is pop round to see Kate and set my mind at rest.

Sue asked a neighbour to mind the children for half an hour while she went out. She hurried straight to Kate's house but when she got there it was in darkness. There was no reply to her knock and it was obvious Kate was not at home. This still didn't prove anything, of course and feeling rather foolish, Sue turned back the way she had come.

She was half-way home when suddenly she noticed something familiar about the loving couple walking towards her. They were arm in arm, oblivious to anything but each other — a pretty sight, except for the fact that the couple were Kate and Dave. Shocked, Sue ducked into a doorway and watched them pass. They continued up the road and disappeared into a pub. Some women might have dashed after them but Sue kept her head. She went quietly home, said not a word to her husband and behaved as normally as possible.

The following week Dave claimed once more to be busy with overtime. Sue made no comment but after he'd left for work she arranged a baby sitter for that evening. She waited until she was sure he would have had time to meet Kate if he was going to and then she set off for the pub. As she'd guessed the couple were there enjoying a drink together. She walked up to them. Dave was flustered but he mumbled out an excuse about having bumped into Kate on his way home.

'Would you like a drink?' he finished weakly.

Sweetly Sue said she would. She waited until he'd paid for it, then she told him that she had seen him with Kate before and she knew what was going on between them. With that she picked up her glass and emptied it all over Kate's head.

'Your bags will be outside the door when you get home,' she told Dave.

Then she rose to her feet and walked out. By the time Dave returned, his cases were neatly stacked on the pavement in front of the house and the chain was on the door. He banged and shouted so much that the neighbours called the police but Sue would not relent. In the end he went back to Kate and Sue got a divorce. Sue never lost her dignity but she was deeply hurt by Dave's betrayal and the treachery of her best friend.

When I looked at her hand I saw a large blurred island

of unfaithfulness spoiling her heart line. It was a great shame because her heart line ended on the mount of Jupiter showing that she herself was a loyal, loving person and deserved better. Interestingly she had a second marriage line high up on her hand showing that she will marry again in later life. Sue refuses to believe this. She says she will never trust a man again. She will of course but it will take a long time before she is ready to trust.

Is your lover married?

It might not be a very romantic way of thinking but if your lover is over the age of about 25, there is a very good chance that he or she is already married. Of course, nobody wants a poisonous, suspicious mind but it has to be said that a great deal of unhappiness is caused by trusting folk believing every word a new lover tells them.

It's the oldest trick in the book of course, pretending to be single when really there's a husband or wife tucked away at home but people still fall for it. Now on this score it has to be said that palmistry can't be 100% accurate but it can give you some useful guidelines.

Look at the marriage lines on his or her hand (women are just as likely as men to pretend they are single). If the first marriage line starts close to the heart line, your new partner will have married very young indeed and if there is no break in the line he or she could well have neglected to get a divorce.

Now look at your own hand. If there is a strong influence line running from inside the mount of Venus across your hand towards your heart line and this influence line is blurred with smaller lines like a trellis over it, it suggests that your life is being strongly influenced by someone who is not free.

Should you find these lines it doesn't necessarily mean that your lover is a liar (although if he possesses a crooked little finger as well, beware), but it would be a good idea

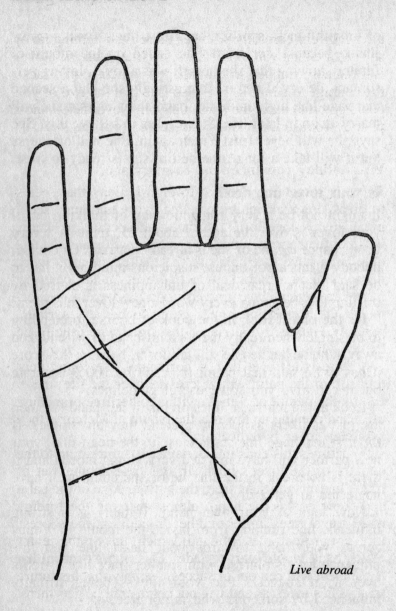

Live abroad

to check very carefully whether there is something he or she is not telling you. Sometimes, it's true, a married lover is genuinely trapped in an unhappy marriage and lacks the courage to admit it. It is also true that the two of you could go on to make the perfect match. Nevertheless most people would rather know the score from the start.

Will holiday romance lead to marriage?

There is something about a foreign holiday that seems to break down all inhibitions and every autumn I see a great many love-lorn returnees, desperate to know whether their torrid sunshine romance will stand the test of time. I have to emphasise that palmistry can't work miracles. You are unlikely to find every detail of every minor entanglement engraved upon your palm. Nevertheless if the relationship is going to be very serious, possibly ending in marriage, the signs will usually be there.

If there is a travel line, a horizontal line found near the base of the palm, which crosses over the life line to end on the mount of Venus, with another line branching off it and running up towards the mount of Mercury, then a foreign lover is indicated.

Sometimes this ends in marriage and emigration to the country of the lover's birth. In this case another set of travel lines would start from the outside edge of the palm and come across the hand, almost meeting the foreign lover travel lines in the middle. In addition the success line (not present in every hand) which runs up the centre of the hand would start to fade. This doesn't mean that the subject will run out of success, simply that his future success lies overseas and will not begin until he gets there.

Are you star crossed lovers?

We all know that the path of true love seldom runs smooth

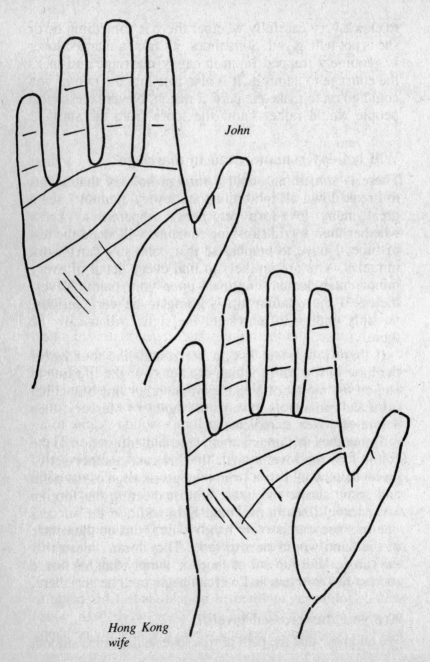

John

*Hong Kong
wife*

but some couples have a rougher ride than others. Like Romeo and Juliet they find that everything and everyone seems against them. Quite often the struggle only serves to strengthen their bond but other romances crumble under the strain. All this, like most other things, can be seen in the hand. If there are lines of opposition present on the palm you can be sure that other people will try to spoil your happiness.

I was reminded of this when I received a pair of hand prints sent to me from Hong Kong. John, the young man who'd written, explained that he wanted to know if he and his girlfriend were ideally suited. The couple had met when John treated himself to a holiday in Hong Kong. By all accounts John was a quiet, steady, hard working sort of man. He'd never been a womaniser and he'd saved for a long time for his dream holiday. Not for John a fortnight of sex and booze in Spain. He genuinely wanted to learn about a different culture.

As it turned out the holiday succeeded better than he'd ever dreamed. Soon after he arrived John met a pretty local girl and within a week they were in love. It seemed too good to be true and being sensible young people they decided not to rush into a firm commitment too soon. Reluctantly they parted when John's holiday came to an end and they continued their courtship by post. Their letters flew backwards and forwards across the world, supplemented by the occasional phone call. They missed each other desperately and John saved every penny so that he could return to Hong Kong.

Now, one year later he was back and the couple's feeling had grown even stronger. They were talking of marriage. Did I think it was a good idea? When I compared their hands I saw that they were very well suited. John was inclined to be jealous but his bride to be was a loyal, sensible girl. They were both warm hearted, passionate types and would undoubtedly be happy together.

That should have been the end of the matter but I could see something else. In addition to these fortunate signs there were other indications that were less promising. Both sets of palms were marked with the clear lines of opposition. The lines of opposition are found on the outer side of the palm between the heart and head lines. If there are more than three lines going diagonally across towards the mount of Venus, then outside influences will try to part the couple. If these lines are accompanied by a break in the heart line and downward disappointment lines, it seems likely that the relationship will founder.

In the case of John and his fiancée there was no sign of a break-up and both young people possessed determined thumbs which would help them stick to their beliefs, but there was no doubt that their feelings for each other would be severely put to the test. Choosing my words carefully, I wrote to John about all my findings. I didn't expect to hear from him again but the following week I received another air-mail letter.

Apparently I was quite right about the opposition to the romance, John explained. Both sets of parents were against the match. Neither of them wanted their children marrying foreigners and living abroad. At one stage his fiancée's father had forbidden her to contact John at all and even threatened to lock her in her room to prevent her from meeting him. The couple remained determined, however, and in the end the parents relented.

Six months later I heard from the couple again. There had been a lot of battles and dramas but they were now married and living in Britain. Neither set of parents had attended the wedding which was sad, but they were blissfully happy and had no regrets. They were certain they'd done the right thing. I'm sure they had.

Will your marriage end in divorce?

Madelaine hadn't come to see me about anything in particular, she said, she was just fascinated by palmistry.

She was an intelligent young woman in her thirties with a wide-awake face and bright, curious eyes and I'm sure her interest was genuine. Yet when I looked at her hand I saw that there was something very wrong in her life and subconsciously at least, I felt that she wanted to know what to do about it.

The most striking feature of her palm was her heart line. To say that it was broken was an understatement. The split was so wide it looked as if she had two separate heart lines next to each other. On her mount of Venus and the mount of Mercury there were grilles showing lack of sexual satisfaction and diagonal lines ran across the mount of Venus towards the thumb hinting at a yearning for physical pleasure.

The bases of Madelaine's fingers were fleshy and she had a full girdle of Venus showing that she was a very passionate lady. From these clues, together with the sexual dissatisfaction indicated, I could tell that sexually there was something badly wrong with Madelaine's marriage. The break in her heart line was so decisive I could see that some major relationship was going to come to an end and when I looked at her marriage line it was broken into three pieces.

There was no doubt in my mind that Madelaine was heading for divorce but I don't like to blurt out such bad news. Instead I mentioned that there were problems with the sexual side of her marriage. Madelaine agreed instantly. It turned out that she was married to a man much older than she was. They were good companions but after a couple of years her husband seemed to lose interest in sex. He was showing his age and was content now to sit by the fire every night in his slippers and retire to bed with a cup of cocoa, to sleep. They had shared a great love in the past and were the proud parents of a highly intelligent little boy but now there was little between them but affection.

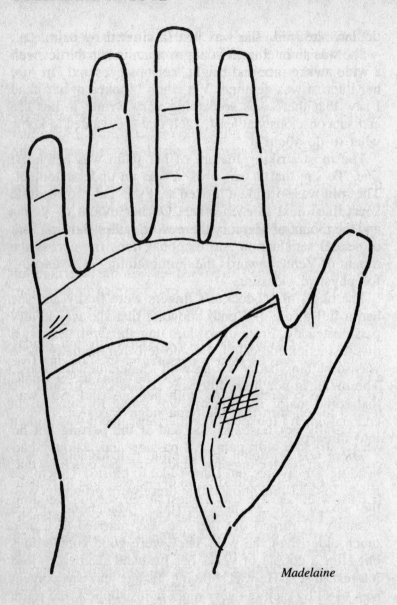

Madelaine

'We're almost like brother and sister these days,' said Madelaine. 'I don't want to hurt him but I do need something more.'

No-one could blame her. She was a healthy young woman after all. What's more there was another, strongly marked marriage line higher up on her hand showing that she was destined to marry again. I advised her for the sake of her child not to do anything hasty, but I added that I could see a second marriage indicated in later life. Two years later Madelaine rang me again.

'I'm sending you a bit of wedding cake Bettina,' she said.

Apparently she had struggled on with the marriage for as long as she could but in the end she met another man at work. They fell madly in love and they were well suited in every way.

For a while Madelaine lived a double life but fundamentally she was an honest person and she couldn't live a lie. Even for the sake of their son she didn't feel it would be right to continue living with her husband. She was forced to tell him that their marriage was over.

Naturally her husband was sad at the parting but he wasn't stricken with pain. All passion and jealousy had gone out of his feelings for Madelaine. So much so that once the initial shock had worn off he was able to remain friends with her. He was a guest at her second wedding and now I believe he is a regular visitor for Sunday lunch.

Few divorces are resolved so amicably of course. Often one partner wants to be free while the other longs for the marriage to continue. Yet the tell tale signs will appear in both hands. A break in the heart line accompanied by a broken marriage line tell their own sad story.

Not all marital problems end in divorce of course. If the marriage line is broken, but continues again after a short gap it suggests that circumstances will part the

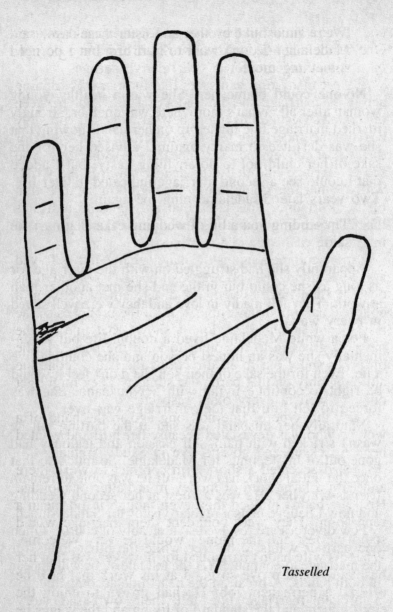

Tasselled

couple for a while but they will get together again in time. One of them might need to work abroad for a period, or go away to care for a sick relative perhaps.

A great many tiny hair lines like little cracks running across the marriage line show a lot of aggravation between the couple. Despite this often they stay together, possibly because the underlying feelings are strong or possibly for the sake of convenience and appearances. Sometimes you see a marriage line that dips deeply towards the wrist, with another line going faintly through it in the direction of the heart line. This is an unusual sign and indicates that the bearer will outlive their partner and go on to marry one of his or her relatives.

A more common sign is the marriage line that is frayed at the end giving the appearance of being tassellated. This occurs when there is a major disagreement between a couple on an important subject. If all the branches of the tassel lean in one direction it shows that one of the partners gives in to the other to keep the peace. If the branches shoot out in all directions the battles continue although only on that particular subject. They might get on very well in every other respect.

I saw this type of line not long ago in the hand of a woman who was devastated because her husband wanted her to pack up and go and live in Saudi Arabia.

He had accepted a short term contract to work there and earn a large sum of money in a matter of months. His wife hadn't minded this, even though it did mean a separation. They were confident their marriage would stand the test and the money would be very welcome. What his wife hadn't bargained for however was that her husband would prove so good at his work that he'd be offered a permanent job. He had grown to enjoy the environment and the standard of living and the wages he was being offered to stay, were the like of which he would never see again. He returned to Britain to urge his wife to emigrate.

To say she wasn't keen was an understatement. She burst into floods of tears when she told me about it. It would mean selling her home and leaving her friends and family, she sobbed. Yet when I looked at her hand there was no sign of divorce. Her marraige line ended in a tassel. What's more all the branches of the tassel pointed in the same direction. I could see that she would eventually do as her husband wanted. And she did. A few months later she popped in to see me during a visit to London. She looked tanned and relaxed and about ten years younger.

'We should have done it years ago, Bettina,' she said. 'It's the best decision we ever made. We couldn't possibly afford to live like that in England and we're having a wonderful time.'

CHAPTER SEVEN:
WILL YOU HAVE CHILDREN?

The girl was sobbing her heart out. She had arrived five minutes before looking reasonably composed but the moment she sat down at the table her lips began to tremble and she burst into tears. She was too distraught even to tell me what was wrong. In the end I made her some tea and sat quietly beside her until at last her sobs subsided.

'Would you like to tell me about it now?' I asked.

The girl blew her nose loudly.

'I'm sorry,' she said, 'I don't know what came over me. I've just come from the doctor you see and he says . . . he says . . .' her eyes filled with tears again but she battled on. '. . . I've got to have a hysterectomy.'

And she started sobbing all over again. After more tea I discovered that she was only 24, and she hadn't yet had any children.

'We've been longing for a family,' she said, 'and now. . . now we won't ever have one.'

'Well let's have a look at your hand,' I said, 'and see what's there.'

She opened her palm and I went straight to her little finger of Mercury to see if there was any sign of children. Children show up in the hand in the form of vertical lines

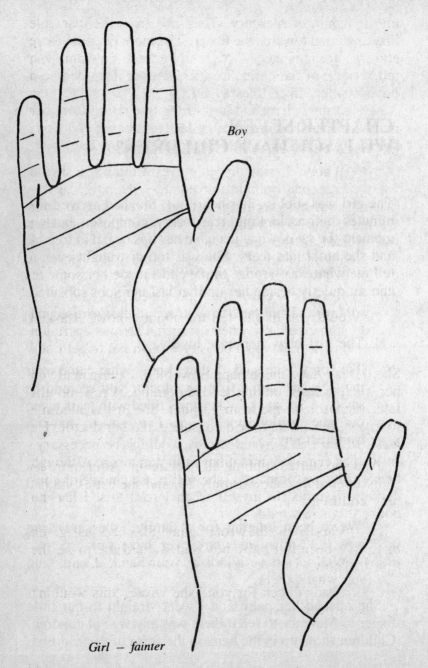

Boy

Girl — fainter

on the mount of Mercury. They rise from the marriage lines and head towards the finger. The more lines the more children are indicated — one child a line. You can even tell the sex of the child. Longer, deeper lines denote a boy, smaller, finer lines a girl.

My unhappy client had one strong line rising from her marriage line showing me that far from being childless, she was destined to be the mother of a healthy baby boy.

'Well now,' I said, 'dry your eyes. I think you should get a second opinion immediately. Don't go agreeing to a hysterectomy just yet. According to your hand you have a child still to come. Only one, but a child all the same.'

She was pleased but incredulous.

'The doctor seemed quite positive.' She said.
'Maybe,' I told her, 'but you are entitled to a second opinion especially when it's such a serious operation as this. I think you'd be very foolish not to get one.'

She left my flat a much happier woman, having made up her mind to insist on that second opinion. A few months later she wrote to me from hospital. She just wanted me to know she said that she'd consulted another doctor. He had told her that a hysterectomy wouldn't be necessary. Instead he removed one of her fallopian tubes. Although her fertility was impaired, she still had a chance of conceiving. I smiled to myself when I read this. I had no doubt that she would.

Two years later she wrote again. She had just given birth to a beautiful baby boy and wanted me to be the first to know.

'If it hadn't been for you,' she wrote, 'this wouldn't have been possible.'

She was overjoyed. It just shows how accurate palmistry can be.

Understanding your child with palmistry

These days modern technology has made it possible to photograph the growing baby while it is still inside its mother's womb. And incredibly enough such pictures reveal that the tiny foetus is perfect in every detail, right down to the lines on its palm. Even before it is born the child bears its own unique life line, head line and heart line.

Interestingly, in the first few weeks of it's life when it is utterly dependent on others and hasn't yet been able to distinguish itself as a separate being, the baby's thumb, the symbol of self and will, is tucked tightly inside its hand. As the baby grows and begins to develop a personality, so it's thumb uncurls.

Between birth and the age of five the hand is growing fast and I believe that this is the time when a parent can most influence the child for good or ill. A quick glance at the palm will help you decide the right path to take.

In general, the longer the head line, the more intelligent the child. If your child has a short head line it indicates a lack of concentration and caring parents can improve this deficiency by making sure that he or she has plenty of stimulating things to do to occupy his or her mind. I have actually seen a child whose head line has grown longer after six months of such 'play'.

When the child's head line is joined to the life line for a short distance it shows a child who is shy and clings to home. Such children need to feel secure at all times and their confidence should be boosted whenever possible. If there is a gap betwen the head line and life line it shows an independent nature and a child that will have a will of its own. There's no need to worry about bringing these little souls out of themselves.

When the head line is long and starts to curve downhill it shows a vivid imagination. Should the curve be very steep the child's imagination is likely to run away with him and he may tell little white lies.

If the hand is full at the side and appears to bulge out in a curve, it shows a creative gift of some kind which should be encouraged. It might be drawing, painting, music, dancing but whatever it is, it will be worthwhile to discover the gift and develop it.

It's very rare to see a child with a double head line but when you do it shows brilliance in academic subjects. Sometimes a double head line appears quite suddenly towards the end of the child's school career. This shows that he or she is a late developer and will do very well in years to come.

The longer the fingers the more methodical the child. His exercise books will be beautifully neat and he will take great pains over everything he does. If the fingers are short this indicates a child in a hurry. Quick and full of energy he is too impatient to worry about carefully formed letters. There is no point in trying to force him to change his ways. He can't go against his nature. A few short but interesting writing exercises might help but don't expect miracles.

A full mount of Venus in a chubby little hand shows a child who needs a lot of affection. Very often these are the children who become jealous when another baby is born. They should be given plenty of cuddles. The child with the narrow mount of Venus is just the opposite. They shrug off displays of sentiment. They are self-contained and less vulnerable but they should be strongly encouraged to share as they could have a tendency towards selfishness.

Lost children

Children bring much joy of course but they can also be the cause of heartache. I shall never forget the case of

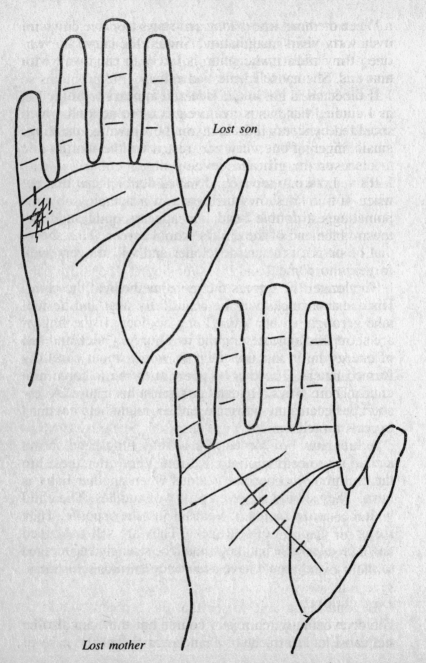

Lost son

Lost mother

a client of mine who had been pining for her child for over forty years. I didn't ever meet this lady. She was one of my clients who sent photocopied hand prints for analysis. She hadn't mentioned any specific problems so I assumed she'd got in touch merely out of curiosity. Yet as I studied her hands I noticed that her heart line was smudged by stress lines and some of these led up to the small finger of Mercury and rested on the mount.

I felt sure that she had some problem connected with a child. Looking down her hand however I saw that the maze of fine lines smoothed out towards the base of the palm suggesting that better times were coming and that the problem was likely to be solved.

As I stared at the prints a clairvoyant picture suddenly formed in my mind and I was looking at a beautiful baby boy. Puzzled, I wrote to the lady asking if she was worried about a child in any way as this seemed to feature very strongly in her hand.

She replied at once with the whole story. She was now nearly seventy years old. Over forty years ago when she was young she found herself pregnant with an illegitimate child. There was no question of the father marrying her and she became an outcast because in those days women in such a predicament were despised. She gave birth to a perfect baby boy but with no one to help her she could not afford to bring him up and reluctantly she agreed to let him go for adoption.

She was assured that he would go to a good home but as the years passed she could never forget him. In fact the older she grew the worse it became. She longed to find her son again and could not bear to go to her grave without explaining to him why she had been forced to give him away.

Beyond being able to see that the problem would be solved eventually, palmistry couldn't give me any further help so I had to try clairvoyance again. This time I was seized with the strong conviction that the woman should contact the Salvation Army as soon as possible. Somehow they would bring about the meeting she longed for. I wrote to her with my suggestions and I heard nothing more for months and months. I had almost forgotten the story. Then the following Christmas I received a Christmas card from her.

Success at last. The Salvation Army had put her in touch with her son. So far they had only spoken on the phone but they would be meeting in a few weeks' time. The boy was now a grown man with a family of his own and the news had given her a new lease of life. She didn't feel lonely any more. She had another family to cherish and she couldn't wait to make up for lost time.

Oddly enough not long after the successful conclusion of this story, I came across a similar case but viewed from a different angle. A young woman came to see me for a general reading and in the course of it I noticed that there was something bothering her and it was to do with a relative. A line representing family influence, ran from inside her life line up towards the heart line and it was covered with diagonal lines showing problems and worry. Yet towards the end the line cleared, showing that the problems would fizzle out.

When I mentioned this the girl explained that she was adopted and lately she had been haunted by the need to find her real mother.

> 'It looks to me as if you will find her,' I said, 'and
> I feel that she is not far away. If I were you I would
> make some discreet enquiries around your family.'

The girl did as I suggested and eventually, her grandmother who was very sick, confided that the woman she had known all her life as her aunt, was in fact her mother. Naturally she was delighted if rather shocked, to know the truth at last but her grandmother had made her promise not to let anyone know that the secret was out. To her frustration she couldn't say a word to her 'aunt'.

The months passed and eventually her grandmother died. Then at the funeral she saw her chance. As the 'aunt' stood sobbing at the graveside, the girl went up and put an arm round her shoulders.

'It's all right, mum, don't cry,' she said.

And from that moment on mother and daughter were able to start their own special relationship.

CHAPTER EIGHT:
TOYBOYS AND BIMBOS

Pat was fifty if she was a day and not a Joan Collins fifty either. Her hair was streaked with grey, her face sagged and her figure was not what it was. Yet there was an attractive sparkle in her eye and she was full of energy.

'You see, Bettina, there's someone else,' she confided with barely contained excitement.

Pat was clearly in love and it wasn't with her husband Ray. Ray was a nice enough man. He was kind and considerate and treated Pat well but he had been slowing down of late, at a time when Pat was revving up.

'Oh Ray's all right,' said Pat dismissively, 'but he's so — so old before his time. Simon makes me feel young again.'

It was a great shame for Ray I thought, but these things happen. I supposed this Simon must be a year or two younger than Pat. Well, as it turned out I was right in thinking Simon was younger but way out in my estimation of how much younger. Simon was just twenty years old — thirty years younger than his new 'girlfriend'. I was staggered. Pat, sedate, middle-aged and ordinary, was the latest in the long line of women to get herself a toyboy.

'I haven't had so much fun in years,' said Pat. 'D'you think it will last?'

I glanced at her. Was she serious? Yes she was serious.

'Well I'd better have a look at your hand,' I told her.

As I suspected, her heart line was feathery with little breaks and downward sloping lines of disappointment. Her relationship would come to an end but by the look of it it would be the first of many and along the way no doubt, Pat would have a lot of fun.

This didn't surprise me. What did surprise me was the fact that Pat had the typical signs of the person who prefers a much younger lover. Her heart line was very thin, it started high on her hand, and near the beginning it rose up into a strange little peak under the small finger of Mercury in the place where you normally find lines indicating children. After the peak it straightened out and crossed her palm in the normal way. In addition her hand was rather hollow.

I've also found these identical signs in the hands of men who prefer to court girls decades younger than themselves.

People with this heart line tend to fear growing old. They either have no children of their own or take little interest in their children if they do, but there is a strongly maternal or paternal element in their feelings for their young lover.

Men of course have been dating and even marrying much younger women for years and the only feeling they seem to arouse in others is admiration and envy. Yet now women are coming into the open and admitting similar tastes it's considered rather shocking.

Well, the people who're shocked are just going to have to get used to it because I'm seeing an increasing number of ladies with toyboys. The experts tell us that, statistically, young men now far outnumber young women, so older ladies could well be in for a bonanza. One of the most extreme cases I heard about was of a grandmother

151

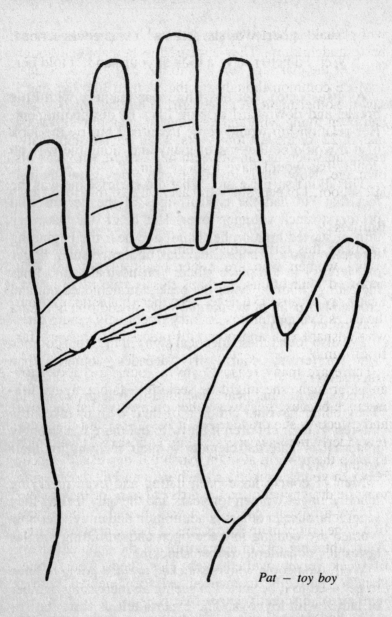

Pat — toy boy

who actually married a boy of 17 who was younger than her grandchildren. They appeared to be happy although whether the marriage survives to this day I have no idea.

More common though are the women like the one I saw the other night. A career girl in her late thirties, she had been living with and keeping an unemployed young man of 22 for the last four years. Their relationship finally broke up when he ran off with her au pair who was his own age. Now she is involved with a boy who has just left school. I expect she will carry on like this for years.

Bimbos

I believe this term comes from America and refers to young women who are rather beautiful but not well endowed with brains. Perhaps this is true in America. I can't say because I've never been there but certainly from the cases I've met in this country, the lovely young girls who ensnare rich and powerful older men are very far from dumb.

There are many reasons why a young girl looks for an older man: she might be seeking a father figure for instance because her own father didn't give her the love and affection she craved. But it has to be said that very few elderly road-sweepers end up with sexy 21-year olds to keep them warm at night. Such liaisons usually occur between young women and rich men and the conclusion must be drawn that often the girls are in it for the money.

I saw a typical case when I was invited to the offices of a large company to read palms at their Christmas party. A breathtaking girl in a beautiful off the shoulder dress of black velvet, wafted over. Her hands were white, slender, perfectly manicured and ornamented with a number of discreetly expensive rings.

She had pointed tips to her fingers, a short heart line curving back towards the mount of Mercury, a narrow mount of Venus, a cross on the mount of Jupiter and a

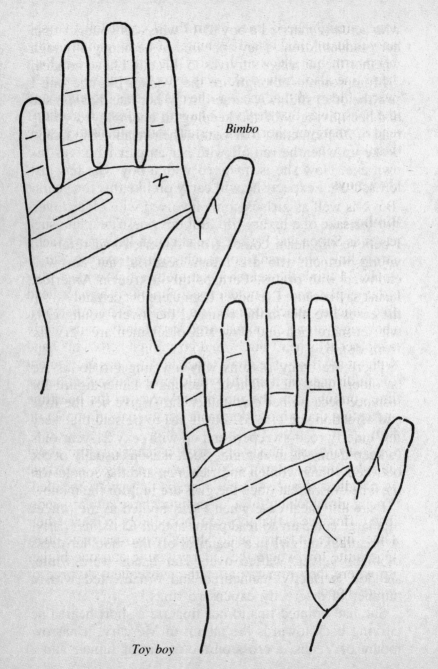

Bimbo

Toy boy

long, straight head line. From this I could tell that she adored luxury and beautiful things, she was neither loving nor warm but she would marry into money. That long head line also showed she was extremely clever. Afterwards I learned that she was the chairman's secretary and the gossip was that they were having an affair. If he didn't end up marrying her I felt certain someone similar soon would.

Toy boys

Boys as well as girls become involved with older lovers for the sake of a luxury life. But this doesn't explain such cases as Simon and Pat because although Pat is not exactly struggling, she hasn't got much cash to spare either.

Here I think the search for a mother figure must play a large part and I would expect Simon to have a head line which is attached to the life line for a short distance, showing a strong emotional need for a family, particularly a mother. His heart line would go straight across his hand without any hint of jealousy since his love has an element of childishness in it and he would have a strong influence line coming from the mount of Venus to his heartline indicating that a more dominant person has an impact on him.

Most of these hands also have a marriage line about halfway up the mount of Mercury denoting a marriage in middle age once the early needs have been fulfilled. Young girls looking for a father figure have similar hands. The difference is that they are more likely to marry their father figure and this usually shows in two marriage lines. One quite low where they marry young and one higher up where they remarry after the subsequent divorce or widowhood.

CHAPTER NINE:
ROYAL LOVE

There is no doubt that most of us are fascinated by royal romances. The delight with which we follow every twist and turn of courtship, the routine denials, the snatched photographs, the first hints that yes something serious might well be brewing — all culminating in that perenially popular spectacular, the royal wedding. It's as riveting as the most dramatic soap opera.

Even after the marriage it doesn't stop. As soon as the honeymoon is over we're bombarded with contradictory stories about the state of the royal relationship. But how can we tell what is true and what is fiction? The press are notoriously untrustworthy in this respect.

The answer strangely enough can be found in the press. Not in the columns of words devoted to the subject but in the photographs that accompany them. There must be thousands and thousands of pictures of members of the royal family waving. Many of them are blurred and unhelpful, but study some of the better ones with a magnifying glass and you will find that the lines on the palms of the hands are clearly visible. From these you can analyse the character almost as well as if the person was sitting there with you.

Even if you can't find a good enough reproduction to see the lines, the shape of the hand, the length and breadth of the fingers, the formation of the thumb will tell you a great deal.

Prince Charles

Prince Charles is a complex character. He can be charming, friendly and amusing. He has a warm heart and cares genuinely about the plight of the underdog. Yet like all of us he has his negative qualities. His long finger of Saturn makes him moody and critical. He is independent, stubborn and he hates to be told what to do. Sometimes he must seem like a Jekyll and Hyde figure.

His palm and fingers are broad at the base showing that he is a very sensuous man and his mount of Venus is full and wide suggesting an affectionate, kind nature. Despite this, he has a stiff thumb reflecting that obstinancy.

His fingers are nice and straight and the outside edge of his palm curves showing honesty and a creative talent but his head line slopes steeply downhill so I expect he suffers from despondency at times.

I think he would make a very good king but sadly I can't see him staying long on the throne, if he reaches it at all. His success line has a distinct break in it showing that there will be a major hitch in his path. What's more his first finger of Jupiter is not long, proving that he would rather follow than lead. He would not be a happy king.

Princess Diana

Princess Diana's hands are soft and her nails short, indicating a highly strung individual. She appears to have flexible tips to her fingers and thumb showing an intuitive, possibly psychic nature. She may not know it but this undoubtedly helps her to get on with people. She does the right thing instinctively.

Her small finger of Mercury is particularly flexible so she is obviously the type of person who hates to be interrupted when she's in the middle of something. She has a straight thumb which is inclined to curve at the bottom hinting at a slightly bossy streak at times and the fact that the first joint is long shows that she can also be stubborn and strong willed. The phalanges of her fingers are straight and even, making her honest and trustworthy, and her Mount of Venus is full so she is also loving and generous.

She has four children indicated in her hand and it looks as if two little princesses will one day join William and Harry in the nursery.

As a couple

This marriage was a mistake for Prince Charles. His head and life lines are joined at the beginning showing a lack of independence and a need for reassurance. He would have been better off with a mature woman who could give him the confidence he needs rather than a very young girl. Yet I feel that Diana will go on to find happiness with another man and probably have two more children. As for Prince Charles he may find personal happiness but I doubt that he will become king.

Prince Andrew

Prince Andrew has large hands with wide palms and broad fingers. Like his brother he is a highly sensuous man. His fingers are long and square showing that he is kind, thoughtful and slow to anger but when he does lose his temper, watch out. Interestingly his first three fingers are almost the same length which indicates that he is a born leader and a good manager of people. The navy is probably the ideal career for him in this respect. Both phalanges on his thumb are long which makes him strong willed and stubborn but this is offset by a keen sense of humour, evidence of which can be found in the wide gap between his heart and head line. He has a wide Mount of Venus showing that he is a loveable man but the life line narrows towards the base suggesting a surprisingly mean streak.

158

Duchess of York

Sarah has very long fingers showing a love of beauty but the tips are firm indicating that she doesn't like to be told what to do. Her first finger of Jupiter is almost as long as the second finger of Saturn, the sign of a natural leader, and her head line is very long. She is an extremely clever girl.

There is a gap between the head line and the life line suggesting an independent nature, a necessity in a sailor's wife I should think. Sarah also has a great sense of humour since the gap between her head line and heart line is wide. Her palm is broad and quite fleshy so she is a passionate girl but her heart line tends to turn upwards suggesting a jealous streak.

As a couple

When these two announced their engagement, I went on television and said that they were mismatched. I'm sorry to say I was proved correct. Sexually I think there is a powerful attraction between them but both have got a heaviness about the thumb that suggests a temper. I think they are an explosive combination and unlikely to reunite.

Some time in the future I would not be surprised if Prince Andrew married a member of some foreign royal family.

Princess Anne

This is a slender hand with long fingers indicating a strong willed person who loves detail and will go to immense trouble to get things right. She has a strong, clear head line showing that she has the ability to bring great patience and concentration to tasks that require thought. She may not be academic but this woman is no fool.

She has a strong thumb and in combination with the rest of her hand it reveals that though she has great patience with animals and abstract problems she can be irritable with people who waste time.

She has a wide Mount of Venus, a sign that this is a woman who needs love and affection and in her second marriage she seems to have found happiness at last.

Prince Edward

Like his sister, Prince Edward has slim hands but the outer side of his palm curves out from the wrist to the base of the small finger of Mercury revealing his well known love of the theatre and show business.

This man may be quiet but he is very independent and knows his own mind. His finger-tips are firm showing that he will not be pushed around or rushed into decisions. His relationships are discreet and although the media would relish a wedding announcement Prince Edward will settle down in his own good time.

CHAPTER TEN:
FAMOUS HANDS

They are always in the newspapers and the gossip columns, those famous faces who flash their photographs about but rarely give interviews, unless that is they've got something to sell. They are part of our lives, as familiar to look at as old friends and yet in reality we know little about them. Oh, we pick up the scraps. We know who they're married to or divorced from. We've heard about their latest movie or record, their greatest triumph, their next ambition. But though they come into our sitting rooms night after night, they might as well be living on another planet.

Yet it's easy to discover the true personalities of the famous. All you have to do is apply the same methods as those used to analyse members of the royal family. Collect a few good photographs of the person you are interested in and study the hands with a strong magnifying glass. You will be amazed at what you discover.

Elizabeth Taylor

Not all sex symbols are sensuous women but Elizabeth Taylor is one of the few. Her palms are broad and the bases of her fingers are fleshy, showing a healthy sex drive. There are lots of lines on her mount of Venus indicating that she is very attractive to members of the opposite sex and she likes to be admired. She is also blessed with a wonderful success line ending in a star under her third finger of Apollo. This is the sign of a person who will have or has had a brilliant career bringing them fame and fortune. True, of course, of Elizabeth.

Unfortunately the side of her hand did not show in the photographs I studied so I was not able to see her marriage lines but I'm sure she will have had quite a series crammed into the small space beneath her fourth finger of Mercury. Her heart line tilts up towards the fingers betraying a jealous and possessive streak and it ends in two branches, one leading off towards the head line and the other to the middle of the fingers. I would say that at one time her heart ruled her head and at another her head ruled her heart.

She is a very independent lady because her head line is completely separate from her life line. She is also extremely clever because this line is double but she probably suffers from depression from time to time since the head line slopes rather steeply.

Despite this she was a wonderful sense of humour because her head line and heart line are quite a distance apart. Her fingers are long and tapering indicating a love of beautiful things yet her joints are knotty, showing a shrewd nature. She is also very strong willed since her thumb is well developed. She craves affection as shown by the wide mount of Venus yet she can also be selfish and occasionally mean because the mount narrows towards the palm.

Interestingly there is a line beginning from inside the life line which goes across the palm up to the heart line. It stops, then goes on to the marriage lines. I would say that soon she will meet someone who will have a terrific impact on her and this meeting will lead to marriage.

Since this line cuts across her success line I feel that the marriage could well coincide with the end of her acting career. I feel she will retire into domestic bliss, not because of the marriage but for health reasons. Suddenly

emotional happiness will give her the excuse she needs
to put her feet up at last.

Bill Clinton

This is a sexy man. The hands are broad and not particularly long, showing a sensuous nature but his fingers are
almost the same size indicating that he can put his views
across with ease. The slightly spatulate fingertips suggest
a love of the outdoors and a flair for open air pursuits
while the palm widens out from the small finger revealing
a love of music and a versatile nature.

Mr Clinton has had his problems lately. With this sensuous
hand he enjoys the good things in life and the glory but he
seems to have miscalculated. His finger joints are not as knotty as those of some other politicians and it could be that he is
not as shrewd as he thinks he is.

His hard finger-tips show that he will not enjoy working with the opposition. I notice that his fourth finger of
Appollo is quite long, indicating a tendency to take a
gamble. Perhaps he could take a massive gamble and call
an election.

Joan Collins

Joan has got a low-set heart line which sweeps in a wide
curve up to the first finger of Jupiter. This upward swing
shows a very possessive and changeable nature. She is
probably very hard to please and she hates to be told
what to do since the tips of her fingers are firm and
unyielding.

She is highly ambitious and there are several lines
reflecting this. One runs up from the head line to the heart
line and suggests that other people have helped her in
her career. She may even have had an unexpected lucky
break at some stage. The other ambition line is double
and runs from the outside edge of her palm up towards
the head and heart lines. This shows that success is very

important to her and that she was absolutely determined to make her name.

As well as being an actress Joan is a natural business-woman. She has a star under the first finger of Jupiter and also under the fourth finger of Mercury. These show firstly that she will accumulate money and secondly that she will make money in business.

She has an excellent memory and a good brain because her head line runs straight across her hand. On the negative side, her thumb is rather heavy for a lady so I would imagine she has a hot temper. She can also be selfish at times because her mount of Venus narrows at the top before widening out.

Like most famous actresses Joan has had her marital troubles but I think there is happiness ahead. There is a strong marriage line high up on her hand indicating a late marriage. This line seems to be stronger than the others and I feel she will fall very deeply in love. Leading to this marriage line is a line which begins from the mount of Venus so I would say that the man who has such an impact on her is already or has already been married. Nevertheless they will share something very special. Before long I can see Joan signing up for a role which will surprise a lot of people.

Michael Jackson

This is an unusual hand. It is extremely long and the heart line shows a changeable and possessive nature. The life line is joined to the head line for a long way indicating strong ties to home and family. I would say this boy didn't want to leave home and remains very attached to one particular member of his family, possibly his mother. His life line is also very long and combined with the other lines on his hand suggests that he will live to a great age.

Oddly enough there is a strange upward peak in his life line which, together with the thick webbing between his thumb and first finger, shows a tremendous love of animals. He is a very honest man, his fingers being straight and even, but he also possesses a noticeably stubborn thumb. He has a double head line and knotty fingers indicating a very good brain and a shrewd outlook.

His Mount of Venus is full showing that he yearns for affection and has a lot of love to give while the pronounced marriage M in the centre of his palm suggests that he will find great happiness in marriage.

Now that he has married Elvis Presley's daughter Lisa I think they will both help each other. Both had unconventional childhoods and both need to know that they are valued for themselves and not their vast fortunes. I'm sure Elvis would had approved thoroughly of the match and just think what a musician their child might turn out to be.

When I look at this hand I get a strong feeling that this man will surprise the world by doing something wonderful for mankind or animals.

Madonna

Madonna's got very long fingers which curve back from the tips. This unusual flexibility shows psychic power and mental and physical agility. Her fingers are also very firm which suggests high energy as well as a tough personality which doesn't take kindly to outside interference.

Her heart line actually curves around towards the back of her hand indicating that her talent was evident from an early age. At the other end it swings up towards the fingers showing that she can be jealous and possessive with those she loves.

There is an unusual cross between her heart and head lines. This is known as the psychic cross and combined with those psychic finger tips Madonna must be very psychic indeed. She may not know that she has this gift but she probably likes or dislikes people on sight and gets premonitions or hunches which always turn out to be right. Her head line slopes steeply hinting that she suf- fers from depression at times yet she is clever and shrewd.

Her success line is wonderful and shoots off in three directions, towards Apollo, Jupiter and Mercury. The line heading to Apollo shows her success in artistic fields but the lines leading to Jupiter and Mercury indicate that she will also do well in some sort of business enterprise. There is a fork at the base of her success line so I would say that she will form a business partnership at some time.

She has more than one marriage line and quite a few relationships indicated in her hand. Her full mount of Venus shows that she is warm and loving but her first finger of Jupiter is long and suggests that she will insist on wearing the trousers. Those long fingers denote a meticulous nature but also a tendency to criticise others. In the future I think she will move more and more into acting and, despite the poor reviews lately, her hand shows acting talent. She must take care of her health, par- ticularly her throat, since she is prone to overstraining it.

Elvis Presley

The late Elvis Presley had an unusual hand. His fingers curved back at the tips reflecting psychic power but the fingers themselves were pointed, showing a fastidious nature. He had a very long thumb but it was thin, indicating a serious weakness in his personality and his head line was not long. Elvis was evidently not the most intellectual of men. Oddly enough his thumb was quite curved suggesting that someone else exerted a terrific influence over him in some way. It could have been his family or an associate, and in fact he was very close to his family, or a member of his family, because his head line and life line were joined for some distance.

Elvis was a very lovable man. He had a full, well developed mount of Venus and the fleshy bases of his fingers show that he had a strong sex drive. He could be very generous and the gaps between his fingers show that money slipped through them like water. It's a good thing he had so much to spare. If he had had an ordinary job and salary he would probably have got himself into serious financial trouble.

All of his fingers lean in towards the second finger of Saturn. When the rest of the fingers lean towards one of them in this fashion it means that the traits associated with that particular finger, dominate the personality.

Saturn is a sombre finger associated with introspection, spiritual matters and melancholy. Under the influence of Saturn, Elvis would have suffered from depression at times and possibly tended to dwell in the past.

Strangely enough, I have seen this combination of factors, the psychic, fastidious fingers, the influence of Saturn and the caring mount of Venus, in the hands of religious leaders. Given a stronger intellect perhaps Elvis would have become an evangelist. As it was I wouldn't be a bit surprised to learn that he dabbled in the occult.

Tammy Wynette

Tammy Wynette has small, delicate hands with slightly pointed fingers. This shows that she loves beautiful things and is fastidious about hygiene. Yet she is not coy when it comes to love. Those pretty fingers are plump at the base, indicating a healthy sex drive, and the lines on her mount of Venus indicate that she is very attractive to the opposite sex not just because of her obvious physical charms. She possesses an invisible magnetism which draws men to her.

Her heart line tilts up towards the fingers suggesting a jealous streak with those she loves, but she is warm hearted and generous as shown by her full mount of Venus. Despite her wealth she always has time for those less fortunate than herself.

Barry Manilow

This is another interesting hand. Barry's heart line ends between fingers of Jupiter and Saturn, showing that he can be jealous and possessive. More unusual is a very rare half moon shaped line on his head line. I have seen this before in the hands of a man who owned an island and I think if he doesn't already own one, Barry will buy an island.

There is also a star on his head line which shows success in his chosen field and judging by the curve at the outside of his hand I would say that this man was talented in several different areas. I feel that he also has acting ability.

His head line is joined to his life line suggesting that he is very close to his family. He has a fantastic sense of humour because there is a wide gap between his head and heart lines. He has a full mount of Venus and fleshy fingers indicating a virile, loving nature and he has a strong marriage line suggesting a long and happy marriage.

There are many fortunate signs in his hand. He has a lot of travel lines at the base of his palm and one of them is linked to a success line leading to the first finger of Jupiter. Obviously Barry travels a lot in the course of his career but this line suggests that he will have overseas business connections. Something to do with property abroad, I should think.

He also has a diamond shape under the small finger of Mercury, a very lucky shape promising success and a lot of money.

All in all there are a great many good things in store for Barry but he must guard his health if he is to enjoy

them to the full. His hand is a mass of tiny lines showing that he is a born worrier and he tends to push himself
too hard. He must learn to relax and take more rest.

Cilla Black

Cilla has square capable hands with knotty fingers. She
may appear daft and giggly but in fact she has a shrewd
brain and would make a good businesswoman. The line
at the base of her fingers slopes steeply downhill indicating
that she has had to struggle to make her way in life, but
she is loving and affectionate as shown by her wide mount
of Venus.

The lines on her palm smooth out towards the wrist
showing that her easiest time is yet to come. Although
she enjoys what's she's doing at the moment, I see her
signing contracts for something quite different in the
future.

Boris Becker

These are very strong hands. The finger tips are firm and
the thumb well developed showing Boris doesn't like being
told what to do and he has a very strong will. That thumb
tends to be heavy so it is likely that he has quite a temper
too.

Despite his youth he is extremely ambitious. Ambition
lines flow from his life line through his success line and
right up to the first finger of Jupiter. His hands are a
mixed shape showing that he is versatile and could
probably make a success of himself in many different
ways.

Although his career is important to him he has a warm
mount of Venus and his heart line turns up towards the
first finger of Jupiter showing that he is idealistic in love.
When he finds the right girl he will put her on a pedestal
and do everything he can to make her happy.

Tom Jones

This is a very sexy man. He has a tremendous Mount of Venus, his fingers are plump and he has a visible girdle of Venus emphasising his sex drive. The line at the base of his fingers slopes down towards the little finger of Mercury showing that he wasn't born with a silver spoon in his mouth and he's had to struggle to reach the top.

The side of his hand is curved showing talent and his long fingers suggest a meticulous nature. Tom will have worked hard on every tiny detail of his act. He hates sloppiness. I don't know whether he had much education or not but this man has a long thumb which indicates a logical mind and good reasoning powers. He may not be an intellectual but he's shrewd and bright. I believe he has lived in America for some years but I can see him returning to Britain to settle permanently in the future.

Clint Eastwood

This man has long, knotty fingers the tips of which are square indicating a shrewd and lively brain. They are also hard so you can tell that he hates to rely on others and will not tolerate interference in his plans.

His head line is long revealing a good brain but it also slopes down into the palm and ends in three distinct branches. This is the sign of someone with a vivid imagination and an artistic flair. It came as no surprise to learn that he had directed his own films as starred in them.

This is a strong, tough personality but the wide Mount of Venus betrays a caring nature and a need for affection.